Barcode in

OUTLAWS, MOBSTERS & CROOKS

OUTLAWS, MOBSTERS & CROOKS

From the Old West to the Internet

VOLUME 2
Computer
Criminals
•
Spies
•
Swindlers
•
Terrorists

Marie J. MacNee
Edited by Jane Hoehner

AN IMPRINT OF GALE

DETROIT · NEW YORK · LONDON

This book is dedicated, with love, to my parents

Outlaws, Mobsters & Crooks: From the Old West to the Internet

by Marie J. MacNee

STAFF

Jane Hoehner, *U•X•L Senior Editor*
Carol DeKane Nagel, *U•X•L Managing Editor*
Thomas L. Romig, *U•X•L Publisher*

Shanna Heilveil, *Production Associate*
Evi Seoud, *Assistant Production Manager*
Mary Beth Trimper, *Production Director*

Jessica L. Ulrich, *Permissions Associate*
Margaret Chamberlain, *Permissions Specialist*

Michelle DiMercurio, *Art Director*
Tracey Rowens, *Senior Art Director*
Cynthia Baldwin, *Product Design Manager*
Barbara J. Yarrow, *Graphic Services Supervisor*

Marco Di Vita, Graphix Group, *Typesetting*

LIBRARY OF CONGRESS CATALOGING-IN-PUBLICATION DATA

MacNee, Marie J.
    Outlaws, mobsters & crooks: from the Old West to the Internet /
Marie J. MacNee : edited by Jane Hoehner.
        p. cm.
    Includes bibliographical references (p.   ) and index.
    Contents: v. 1. Mobsters, racketeers and gamblers, robbers — v.
2. Computer criminals, spies, swindlers, terrorists — v. 3. Bandits
and gunslingers, bootleggers, pirates.
    Summary: Presents the lives of seventy-five North American
criminals including the nature of their crimes, their motivations,
and information relating to the law officers who challenged them.
    ISBN 0-7876-2803-4 (set : acid-free paper). — ISBN 0-7876-2804-2
(vol. 1 : acid-free paper). — ISBN 0-7876-2805-0 (vol. 2 : acid
free paper). —ISBN 0-7876-2806-9 (vol. 3 : acid-free paper)
    1. Criminals—North America—Biography—Juvenile literature.
[1. Criminals.]   I. Hoehner, Jane.   II. Title.   III. Title:
Outlaws, mobsters, and crooks.
HV6245.M232   1998
354.1'097—DC21   98-14861
                                                                 CIP
                                                                  AC

Contents

Volume 1

VOLUME 2

For reasons that have never been explained, a group of five young men, led by Rufus Buck, embarked on a thirteen-day crime spree in July 1895.

At a time when women didn't wear men's clothing, frequent bars, or appear in public drunk, Calamity Jane earned a reputation as an outlaw because she did so—and then some.

A likable and intelligent young man, Cassidy belonged to a group of outlaws known as the Wild Bunch and participated in a number of successful bank and train robberies in the American West at the end of the nineteenth century.

At a time when both outlaws and lawmen built reputations on their ability to handle a gun, Curly Bill made a name for himself as a superior shootist.

Best remembered for his role in the shootout at the O.K. Corral, Earp, a man of the law, was branded as both a hero and a killer.

Both a ruthless killer and a religious family man, bankrobber Jesse James earned a reputation as the Robin Hood of the West before he was betrayed by a member of his gang.

An expert rider and crack shot, Starr was a horse and cattle thief who earned a reputation as the female Jesse James.

A former Texas Ranger, Stoudenmire has been remembered as one of the most sensational lawmen of the West—and as a man who sometimes stood on the wrong side of the law.

A gifted soldier and ruthless killer, Villa spent a decade fighting for Mexico's freedom during the Mexican Revolution.

Hot tempered and unpredictable, Alterie had a Wild West approach to bootlegging in Prohibition-era Chicago.

Six Italian-born brothers, known as "the Terrible Gennas," built a bootlegging empire in Chicago during the early years of Prohibition.

Reader's Guide

"History is nothing more than a tableau of crimes and misfortunes," wrote eighteenth-century French writer Voltaire. There certainly is more to history than criminal deeds, misdemeanors, and misfortunes, but these offenses do offer fascinating lessons in history. The life stories of outlaws provide a glimpse into other times and other places, as well as provocative insight into contemporary issues.

WHO'S INCLUDED

Outlaws, Mobsters & Crooks: From the Old West to the Internet presents the life stories of seventy-three outlaws who lived (or committed crimes) in North America from the seventeenth century to the present day—from Blackbeard, the British-born pirate who terrorized the Carolina coast, to terrorist Timothy McVeigh.

Everyone's familiar with Bonnie and Clyde, Butch Cassidy, and Al Capone. But how many know the *whole* story: what their childhoods were like, what their first crime was, who worked with them—and against them—and how they ended up? *Outlaws, Mobsters & Crooks* offers a thorough and provocative look at the people and events involved in these stories.

Familiar figures such as Jesse James and Billy the Kid are present, as are lesser-known outlaws whose careers reveal much about the times in which they lived. Cattle Kate, for instance, was little more than a cattle rustler, but her story provides insight into the cattle wars of nineteenth-century Nebraska and the tensions that led to the Lincoln County War. Also included are outlaws such as Calamity Jane, whose main crime was unconventionality, and lawmen who sometimes stood on the wrong side of the law. The many men and women who have been labeled outlaws over the course of three centuries cannot all be profiled in one three-volume work. But those whose stories are told in *Outlaws, Mobsters & Crooks* include some of the best known, least known, weirdest, scariest, most despised, and least understood outlaws. In short, this work is intended as an overview of North American criminals—a jumping-off point for further inquiry.

LEGENDS, MYTHS, AND OUTRIGHT LIES

Many of the men and women profiled have been surrounded by legends that have grown to enormous proportions, making it very difficult to separate fact from fiction: Billy the Kid killed one man for every year of his life (he probably killed no more than six men); Jesse James lived to old age as a gentleman farmer (he was shot in the back of the head by Robert Ford at the age of thirty-four); Black Hand extortionists could bring bad luck to their victims simply by giving them "the evil eye" (they brought them bad luck, all right, but it was usually accomplished with a gun). In some cases, legends have fed on the published accounts of the criminals themselves—or the lawmen who pursued them. Some are accurate first-person accounts. Others are sensational exaggerations of true events—or wholesale fabrications. *Outlaws, Mobsters & Crooks* attempts to present a fair and complete picture of what is known about the lives and activities of the seventy-three outlaws profiled. When appropriate, entries mention the myths, unconventional theories, and alternate versions of accepted history that surround a particular outlaw—without suggesting they are truthful or fact-based.

ARRANGEMENT AND PRESENTATION

Outlaws, Mobsters & Crooks is arranged into three volumes. To enhance the usefulness of these volumes, the seventy-three entries have been grouped into ten categories: Mobsters, Racketeers and Gamblers, and Robbers (Volume 1); Computer Criminals, Spies, Swindlers, and Terrorists (Volume 2); and Bandits and Gunslingers, Bootleggers, and Pirates (Volume 3). Within each category, entries—which range from three to eleven pages in length—are arranged alphabetically by the outlaw's last name. The only exceptions to this arrangement are those outlaws who are listed by their "common" name, such as Billy the Kid or Black Bart; these entries are listed alphabetically by the first letter in that name. Aliases and birth names are presented when available. Each entry includes the birth and death dates of the subject (or the period during which he, she, or the gang was active).

Entries are lively, easy to read, and written in a straightforward style that is geared to challenge—but not frustrate—students. Difficult words are defined within the text; some words also include pronunciations. Technical words and legal terms are also explained within entries, enabling students to learn the vocabulary appropriate to a particular subject without having to consult other sources for definitions.

WHAT'S INSIDE

A detailed look at what they did, why they did it, and how their stories ended. Entries focus on the entire picture—not just the headline news—to provide the following sorts of information:

• **Personal background:** interesting details about the subject's family, upbringing, and youth

• **Crimes and misdeeds:** an in-depth look at the subject's outlaw history

• **Aftermath:** from jail time, to legal and illegal executions, to mysterious disappearances, entries relate what happened after the dirty deeds were done

• **A look at the other side of the law:** Many entries also provide extensive information on the other side of the law, for example, the brilliant astronomer who tracked a West German hacker, the FBI agents who hounded John Dillinger and Al Capone, and the frontier judge who earned the nickname "the hanging judge."

ADDED FEATURES

Outlaws, Mobsters & Crooks includes a number of additional features that help make the connection between people, places, and historic events.

• A timeline at the beginning of each volume provides a listing of outlaw landmarks and important international events.

- Sidebars provide fascinating supplemental information, such as sketches of criminal associates, profiles of law enforcement officials and agencies, and explanations of the political and social scenes of the era, for example, the anti-communist hysteria that consumed the United States at the time of the Rosenberg trial. Sidebars also offer a contemporary perspective of people and events through excerpts of letters written by the outlaw profiled, citations from newspapers and journals of the day, and much more.

- Quotes—both by and about the outlaw—offer revealing insights into their lives and times.

- 117 photographs and illustrations bring the outlaws to life.

- Suggestions for related books and movies—both fictional and fact-based—are liberally sprinkled throughout the entries.

- A list of sources for further reading at the end of each entry lists books, newspaper and magazine articles, and Internet addresses for additional and bibliographical information.

- A comprehensive index at the end of each volume provides easy access to the people, places, and events mentioned throughout *Outlaws, Mobsters & Crooks: From the Old West to the Internet.*

SPECIAL THANKS

The author would like to thank U•X•L Senior Editor Jane Hoehner, Permissions Associate Jessica L. Ulrich, and the research staff—particularly Maureen Richards—of Gale Research for their invaluable help and guidance. The author would also like to thank the staff of the Grosse Pointe Library for their gracious assistance.

COMMENTS AND SUGGESTIONS

We welcome your comments on this work as well as suggestions for personalities to be featured in future editions of *Outlaws, Mobsters & Crooks: From the Old West to the Internet.* Please write: Editors, *Outlaws, Mobsters & Crooks,* U•X•L, 835 Penobscot Building, Detroit, Michigan, 48226-4094; call toll-free: 1 (800) 877-4253; or fax (313) 877-6348.

Outlaws Alphabetically

Italic number indicates volume number

Timeline

Spring 1718: Edward Teach—also known as **Blackbeard**—and his crew of pirates blockade the city of Charleston, South Carolina.

November 1718: Thomas Spotswood, the governor of Virginia, issues a proclamation offering rewards for the capture—dead or alive—of **Blackbeard** and his shipmates.

November 22, 1718: A navy crew led by Lieutenant Robert Maynard attacks **Blackbeard**'s pirate ship near the Carolina coast. The severed head of Blackbeard is hung from the bowsprit of the navy ship.

1720: Captain Woodes Rogers, the governor of the Bahamas, issues a proclamation naming Calico Jack Rackam, **Anne Bonny,** and Mary Read as enemies of England.

May 9, 1800: Joseph Baker and two other pirates are hanged in a public execution in Philadelphia, Pennsylvania.

March 11, 1831: Charles Gibbs and Thomas G. Wansley are convicted of murder and piracy in New York.

March 19, 1831: An Englishman named Edward Smith commits the first bank heist in American history when he robs the City Bank in New York City.

April 22, 1831: Pirates **Charles Gibbs** and Thomas G. Wansley are hanged on Ellis Island in New York in front of thousands of onlookers.

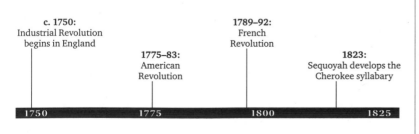

c. 1750:
Industrial Revolution begins in England

1775–83:
American Revolution

1789–92:
French Revolution

1823:
Sequoyah develops the Cherokee syllabary

| 1750 | 1775 | 1800 | 1825 |

July 11, 1859: Gold thief **Richard Barter** is shot and killed by Sheriff J. Boggs in the California foothills.

1861: Shortly after the Civil War breaks out, **Elizabeth Van Lew,** a Union sympathizer who lives inside the Confederacy, begins to send information about the Southern war effort to Northern officers.

February 13, 1866: Jesse James and the James-Younger Gang rob the Clay County Savings and Loan Bank in Liberty, Missouri.

April 5, 1866: Bill Miner enters San Quentin penitentiary after being convicted of armed robbery. He is released after serving a little more than four years of his sentence.

January 23, 1871: Bill Miner and two accomplices rob a California stagecoach using stolen guns. He returns to San Quentin the following June.

October 9, 1871: Swindler **Sophie Lyons** is convicted of grand larceny and sentenced to serve time in Sing Sing prison.

December 19, 1872: Sophie Lyons escapes from Sing Sing prison using a forged key.

1873: The James-Younger Gang commits its first train robbery.

1874: Gunslinger **Clay Allison** commits his first recorded killing.

July 26, 1875: Charles Boles—better known as **Black Bart**—commits the first in a series of stagecoach robberies near Copperopolis, California.

August 3, 1877: Black Bart robs his fourth stagecoach, leaving behind a poem signed "Black Bart, the PO 8 [poet]."

1878: Martha Jane Cannary—known as **Calamity Jane**—acts as a nurse during a smallpox epidemic in Deadwood, Dakota Territory.

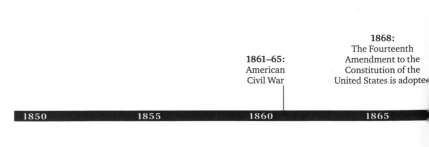

1861–65:
American
Civil War

1868:
The Fourteenth
Amendment to the
Constitution of the
United States is adopted

1850	1855	1860	1865

Spring 1878: Sam Bass and his gang stage four train holdups around Dallas, Texas.

April 1, 1878: William Bonney—also known as **Billy the Kid**—participates in an ambush that kills Sheriff William Brady in Lincoln County, New Mexico.

July 15, 1878: Texas Rangers wound and capture robber **Sam Bass** in Round Rock, Texas.

1879: Bartholomew "Bat" Masterson is appointed deputy U.S. marshal.

October 7, 1879: The second James Gang robs a train near Glendale, Missouri, of $35,000.

December 1879: Wyatt Earp arrives in lawless Tombstone, Arizona, and is soon joined by brothers James, Morgan, Virgil, and Warren.

July 14, 1880: Bill Miner is released from San Quentin prison after serving nine years for stagecoach robbery. He returns to the California prison the following year.

April 11, 1881: Dallas Stoudenmire becomes marshal of El Paso, Texas.

May 13, 1881: Convicted of murder, **Billy the Kid** is sentenced to hang.

May 25, 1881: Livestock rustler **Curly Bill,** otherwise known as William Brocius, is shot in the mouth during an argument with lawman William Breakenridge.

July 14, 1881: Sheriff Pat Garrett shoots and kills **Billy the Kid.**

October 26, 1881: Wyatt Earp and brothers Morgan and Virgil, joined by Doc Holliday, confront the Clantons and McLauries at the O.K. Corral. The gunfight leaves three men dead.

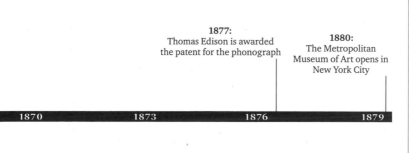

1877:
Thomas Edison is awarded the patent for the phonograph

1880:
The Metropolitan Museum of Art opens in New York City

1870   1873   1876   1879

April 3, 1882: Jesse James dies in St. Joseph, Missouri, after fellow outlaw Robert Ford shoots him in the back of the head.

June 1882: Pressured by city officials, **Dallas Stoudenmire** resigns from his post as marshal of El Paso.

September 18, 1882: Dallas Stoudenmire is shot and killed during a saloon brawl.

1883: Belle Starr is the first woman ever to be tried for a major crime in Judge Isaac Parker's infamous "court of the damned."

November 1883: Black Bart is captured in San Francisco, California. He pleads guilty to robbery and is sentenced to six years at San Quentin penitentiary.

October 6, 1885: Swindler **Ellen Peck** is convicted of forging a document to obtain $3,000 from the Mutual Life Insurance Company of New York. She is sentenced to four-and-a-half years in prison.

July 3, 1887: Clay Allison dies when he is run over by a freight wagon.

November 3, 1887: Robert Leroy Parker—better known as **Butch Cassidy**—and members of the McCarty Gang botch a robbery of the Denver and Rio Grande Express train in Colorado.

1889: Maverick calves stolen from the herds of Wyoming cattle barons find their way into the corral of **Cattle Kate**.

February 3, 1889: Belle Starr is ambushed and killed near her home in the Indian Territory by an unidentified gunman.

March 30, 1889: Butch Cassidy and other gang members rob the First National Bank of Denver of $20,000 in bank notes.

July 20, 1889: Cattle baron Albert J. Bothwell organizes a group to put an end to **Cattle Kate** and James Averill's cattle rustling. Watson and Averill are lynched.

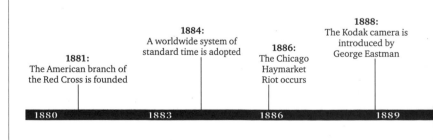

1881:
The American branch of the Red Cross is founded

1884:
A worldwide system of standard time is adopted

1886:
The Chicago Haymarket Riot occurs

1888:
The Kodak camera is introduced by George Eastman

1880　　　1883　　　1886　　　1889

1890s: Black Hand Society extortionists prey on Italian immigrants by threatening violence if their victims do not pay. The Black Hand reign of terror continues for approximately thirty years in Italian Harlem.

1890s: Swindler **Sophie Lyons** opens the New York Women's Banking and Investment Company with fellow con artist Carrie Morse. Before closing, the operation collects at least $50,000 from unsuspecting victims.

November 4, 1890: Marion Hedgepeth and other gangsters rob the Missouri Pacific train near Omaha, Nebraska. The following week they strike the Chicago, Milwaukee & St. Paul train just outside of Milwaukee, Wisconsin.

1892: After a long delay, **Marion Hedgepeth** is tried and convicted of train robbery. He is sentenced to serve twelve to twenty-five years in the state penitentiary.

1894: Posing as the wife of a Danish navy officer, **Ellen Peck** collects more than $50,000 from various banks.

July 4, 1894: Butch Cassidy is tried for cattle rustling. He is convicted and imprisoned.

July 28, 1895: Five young men, known as the **Buck Gang,** begin a murderous thirteen-day crime spree in the Indian Territory to the west of Arkansas.

August 10, 1895: All five members of the **Buck Gang** are captured and taken into custody.

1896: Calamity Jane works for an amusement company in Minneapolis, Minnesota, dressed as an army scout.

January 19, 1896: Butch Cassidy is released from the Wyoming State Penitentiary.

July 1, 1896: Rufus Buck and four other **Buck Gang** members are executed in a mass hanging at Fort Smith, Arkansas.

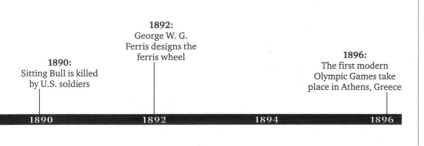

1890:
Sitting Bull is killed
by U.S. soldiers

1892:
George W. G.
Ferris designs the
ferris wheel

1896:
The first modern
Olympic Games take
place in Athens, Greece

1890   1892   1894   1896

1897: Cassie Chadwick is released from prison after serving three years for fraud. She soon begins to swindle banks by claiming to be the illegitimate daughter of millionaire Andrew Carnegie.

1899: Pearl Hart and Joe Boot rob the Globe stage in the Arizona Territory—in what is recognized as the last American stagecoach robbery.

1900: When Mads Albert Sorenson dies in Chicago, his wife, **Belle Gunness,** is suspected of foul play.

May 1900: Found living in a brothel, **Calamity Jane** travels to Buffalo, New York, where she takes a job performing in a Western show at the Pan-American Exposition.

September 25, 1900: Union spy **Elizabeth Van Lew** dies in Richmond, Virginia, at the age of seventy-two.

July 3, 1901: Butch Cassidy and the Wild Bunch raid the Great Northern Flyer train near Wagner, Montana. It is the gang's final heist.

December 19, 1902: Pearl Hart leaves Yuma prison following an eighteen-month imprisonment.

August 1, 1903: Ravaged by alcoholism, **Calamity Jane** dies near Deadwood, Dakota Territory.

September 13, 1904: Bill Miner and others rob an express train outside of Vancouver, Canada.

December 7, 1904: Swindler **Cassie Chadwick** is arrested in New York. She is later convicted of six counts of fraud and sentenced to ten years in the Ohio State Penitentiary.

1905: Wealthy Brooklyn, New York, butcher Gaetano Costa refuses to pay a **Black Hand** extortionist and is shot to death in his shop.

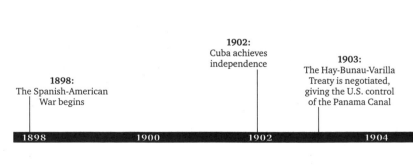

1902:
Cuba achieves independence

1903:
The Hay-Bunau-Varilla Treaty is negotiated, giving the U.S. control of the Panama Canal

1898:
The Spanish-American War begins

| 1898 | 1900 | 1902 | 1904 |

1906: Cassie Chadwick dies at the age of forty-eight in the prison hospital at Ohio State Penitentiary.

1906: Belle Gunness begins to place personal ads in newspapers in Chicago and other cities in the Midwest to lure wealthy men to her Indiana farm.

1908: Joseph Weil works with Fred "the Deacon" Buckminster to trick clients into paying to have them paint buildings with a phony waterproofing substance. It is the first in a series of scams committed by Weil over the next twenty-five years.

April 28, 1908: After the farmhouse belonging to **Belle Gunness** burns to the ground, authorities discover the decapitated corpse of a woman in the ruins.

May 22, 1908: Ray Lamphere, **Belle Gunness**'s farmhand, is tried and acquitted of murder. Convicted of arson, he is sentenced to up to twenty years in prison.

1910: The six **Genna brothers**—later known as "the Terrible Gennas"—arrive in the United States from Marsala, Sicily.

January 1, 1910: Former train robber **Marion Hedgepeth** is killed by a policeman during an attempted saloon robbery.

February 22, 1911: Bill Miner commits his last train robbery at Sulfur Springs, Georgia, at the age of sixty-four.

1912: Mexican General Victoriano Huerta condemns soldier **Pancho Villa** to death. A stay of execution is later issued.

1912: The **Genna brothers** become involved in **Black Hand Society** activities in Chicago.

November 6, 1912: Eleven members of New York's Hudson Dusters Gang ambush rival gangster **Owney Madden** at a Manhattan dance hall. Left for dead, Madden lives.

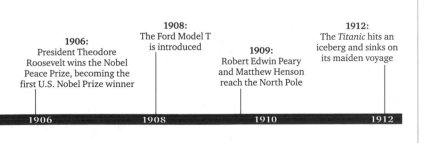

1906:
President Theodore Roosevelt wins the Nobel Peace Prize, becoming the first U.S. Nobel Prize winner

1908:
The Ford Model T is introduced

1909:
Robert Edwin Peary and Matthew Henson reach the North Pole

1912:
The *Titanic* hits an iceberg and sinks on its maiden voyage

1906   1908   1910   1912

1913: Forty-one-year-old **Diamond Joe Esposito** spends $65,000 to celebrate his marriage to sixteen-year old Carmela Marchese.

1913: *Why Crime Does Not Pay,* the autobiography of veteran swindler **Sophie Lyons,** is published.

September 2, 1913: Veteran stagecoach and train robber **Bill Miner** dies in a prison hospital in Georgia.

November 28, 1914: Owney Madden kills rival New York gangster Patsy Doyle. Sentenced to twenty years for the murder, he is released after serving nine years.

March 9, 1916: Pancho Villa and a gang of Villistas (followers of Villa) attack a small New Mexico border town and military camp, killing seventeen Americans.

1917: The obituary of stagecoach robber **Black Bart** appears in New York newspapers. Some people suspect that the death notice is a hoax engineered by the outlaw.

May 24, 1918: Bugs Moran is convicted of armed robbery and sentenced to serve time at Joliet State Prison in Illinois.

November 24, 1918: Bank robbers **Margie Dean** and husband Dale Jones are shot to death in their car by police near Los Angeles, California.

1919: Racketeer **Arnold Rothstein** masterminds the "Black Sox scandal"—the fixing of the 1919 World Series.

1919: Al Capone, a gunman for New York's notorious James Street Gang, moves to Chicago to escape arrest on a murder charge.

December 1919: Swindler **Charles Ponzi** launches an eight-month get-rich-quick scam using international postal reply coupons.

1914:
World War I begins

1917:
Russian Revolution

1918:
Kaiser Wilhelm II of Germany
abdicates the throne

1914   1916   1918   1920

1920: A grand jury meets in Chicago to investigate the 1919 Black Sox scandal.

1920: The **Genna brothers** turn Chicago's Little Italy into a vast moonshine operation.

May 8, 1924: Former swindler **Sophie Lyons** is attacked in her home. She dies later that evening in Grace Hospital in Detroit.

September 6, 1924: John Dillinger and Edgar Singleton rob an Indiana grocer, for which Dillinger is later sentenced to ten to twenty years in prison.

November 10, 1924: Chicago gangster Charles Dion O'Banion is assassinated in his North Side flower shop.

1925: Charles Ponzi is released from prison after serving four years in a Plymouth, Massachusetts, prison for mail fraud.

January 12, 1925: O'Banion gangsters attempt to ambush **Al Capone** by firing into the gangster's limousine. Capone is not injured.

January 24, 1925: Johnny Torrio, who rules Chicago's South Side bootlegging empire with **Al Capone,** is ambushed by rival gangsters.

June 13, 1925: A car filled with Genna gunmen ambushes **Bugs Moran** and Vincent "the Schemer" Drucci on Michigan Avenue in downtown Chicago. Both are wounded—but not killed.

September 20, 1926: Chicago gangster **Hymie Weiss** leads a squad of North Side gangsters in an attempt to ambush **Al Capone** at the Hawthorne Inn, the gangster's Cicero headquarters. Although more than one thousand bullets rip into the building, Capone escapes without injury.

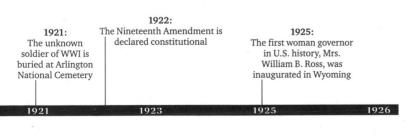

1921:
The unknown soldier of WWI is buried at Arlington National Cemetery

1922:
The Nineteenth Amendment is declared constitutional

1925:
The first woman governor in U.S. history, Mrs. William B. Ross, was inaugurated in Wyoming

1921 1923 1925 1926

1927: Wanted in connection with a robbery, **Ma Barker**'s boy, Herman, commits suicide during a battle with police in Wichita, Kansas.

1928: The **Purple Gang** trial ends the Cleaners and Dyers War in Detroit.

March 21, 1928: Joe Esposito dies near his Chicago home when machine-gunners fire on him from a car. Esposito is struck by fifty-eight bullets.

November 4, 1928: Racketeer **Arnold Rothstein** is shot at the Park Central Hotel in New York. He dies two days later.

1929: Twenty-year old **Irene Schroeder** abandons her husband to run away with Walter Glenn Dague. The couple soon rob a number of stores and small banks.

January 13, 1929: Former lawman **Wyatt Earp** dies in California at the age of eighty, having outlived his four brothers.

February 14, 1929: Members of **Al Capone**'s gang masquerade as policemen raiding a garage on North Clark Street in Chicago. The St. Valentine's Day Massacre leaves seven people dead.

June 13, 1929: Legs Diamond and his enforcer, Charles Entratta, kill two men at the Hotsy Totsy Club, a Manhattan speakeasy.

1930s: Meyer Lansky, Lucky Luciano, and others work together to help solidify a nationwide crime syndicate. Many former bootleggers and members of gangs such as Detroit's **Purple Gang** join the national syndicate.

November 17, 1930: Sam Battaglia robs Mrs. William Hale Thompson—the wife of the governor of Illinois—of more than $15,000 in jewels.

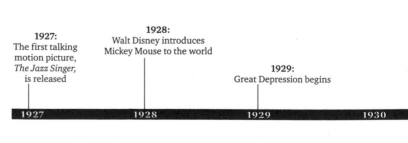

1927:
The first talking motion picture, *The Jazz Singer,* is released

1928:
Walt Disney introduces Mickey Mouse to the world

1929:
Great Depression begins

| 1927 | 1928 | 1929 | 1930 |

1931: Veteran gangster Joe "the Boss" Maseria is assassinated in a restaurant in Coney Island, New York. **Bugsy Siegel** is among the hitmen.

February 23, 1931: Irene Schroeder is executed at Rockview penitentiary in Pennsylvania. Her partner, Walter Glenn Dague, is executed a few days later.

April 1931: Legs Diamond is shot several times in a drive-by ambush. He survives.

June 1931: Federal officials charge Chicago gangster **Al Capone** with income tax evasion.

September 16, 1931: Three unarmed men are shot to death by **Purple Gang** mobsters. The incident is known as the Collingwood Manor Massacre.

October 1931: Al Capone is convicted of income tax evasion and sentenced to eleven years in prison.

December 17, 1931: Legs Diamond is shot dead by rival gangsters in his hotel room in Albany, New York.

1932: Gangster **Owney Madden** is released from Sing Sing prison. Later that year he is jailed again for parole violation. Released, he retires from the New York underworld.

February 2, 1932: Clyde Barrow is paroled from Eastham prison farm in Ohio—vowing that he will die before returning to prison. Barrow rejoins **Bonnie Parker** and the two embark on a two-year crime spree.

February 8, 1932: Dutch Schultz's gunmen murder Vincent Coll as Coll makes a call from a phone booth.

1931:
The *Star-Spangled Banner* becomes the national anthem of the United States

1932:
Amelia Earhart becomes the first woman to cross the Atlantic in a solo flight

1931   1932

1933: FBI agent Melvin Purvis arrests Chicago gangster **Roger Touhy** for the kidnapping of millionaire William A. Hamm, Jr. Touhy is cleared of the kidnapping, which was engineered by members of the Barker-Karpis Gang.

1933: Murder, Inc.—an enforcement division of the national crime syndicate—is formed under the leadership of **Louis Lepke.**

May 22, 1933: Thanks in part to a petition by friends and relatives, **John Dillinger** is released early from the Michigan City prison in Indiana.

July 22, 1933: Machine Gun Kelly and Albert Bates kidnap oil millionaire Charles F. Urschel from his Oklahoma City mansion.

September 26, 1933: Memphis, Tennessee, police detectives capture kidnappers **Machine Gun Kelly** and Albert Bates.

September 26, 1933: Using guns smuggled by **John Dillinger,** ten prisoners escape from the Michigan City penitentiary in Indiana. Bank robber Harry Pierpont is among the escaped convicts.

1934: Swindler **Charles Ponzi** is deported to Italy as an undesirable alien.

January 1934: The Dillinger Gang falls apart when police arrest **John Dillinger** and others in Tucson, Arizona. Dillinger is extradited to Indiana.

May 23, 1934: Bonnie and Clyde are killed by lawmen as they drive down a back road near Arcadia, Louisiana.

July 22, 1934: Tipped off by the "Lady in Red," FBI agents apprehend **John Dillinger** as he leaves Chicago's Biograph Theater. The gangster, who is recognized as Public Enemy Number One, is shot dead.

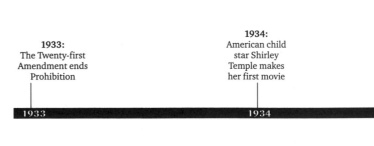

1933:
The Twenty-first Amendment ends Prohibition

1934:
American child star Shirley Temple makes her first movie

1933   1934

1935: Two Gun Alterie is called as a government witness in the income tax evasion trial of Ralph "Bottles" Capone (brother of **Al Capone**).

1935: New York mayor Fiorello LaGuardia and district attorney Thomas E. Dewey join forces to destroy **Dutch Schultz**'s slot machine empire. Schultz later vows to kill Dewey.

1935: Ray Hamilton, a former associate of outlaws **Bonnie and Clyde,** is put to death in the electric chair.

January 8, 1935: Arthur "Doc" Barker, wanted for killing a night watchman, is captured in Chicago by FBI agent Melvin Purvis.

January 16, 1935: After a four-hour gun battle, **Ma Barker** and her son Fred are killed by lawmen near Lake Weir, Florida.

July 18, 1935: Former bootlegger **Two Gun Alterie** is killed in a machine-gun ambush.

October 23, 1935: Dutch Schultz, a member of the board of the national crime syndicate, is ambushed in a Newark, New Jersey, chophouse with three associates.

1936: Juliet Stuart Poyntz, an American communist and Soviet spy, is seen in Moscow in the company of fellow American and convicted spy George Mink.

May 1936: Alvin Karpis, a member of the Barker-Karpis Gang, is captured in New Orleans, Louisiana. FBI director J. Edgar Hoover personally places him under arrest.

1939: Gangster **Frank Costello** is tried in New Orleans, Louisiana, on charges of tax evasion. The government loses its case because of lack of evidence.

August 24, 1939: Racketeer **Louis Lepke** surrenders to the FBI through newspaper columnist Walter Winchell.

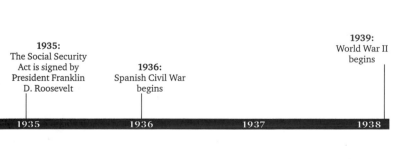

1935:
The Social Security Act is signed by President Franklin D. Roosevelt

1936:
Spanish Civil War begins

1939:
World War II begins

1935   1936   1937   1938

1940: Joseph Weil is sentenced to three years in prison for a mail-fraud charge involving phony oil leases. It is the veteran swindler's final conviction.

October 9, 1942: Roger Touhy and six other prisoners escape from Joliet penitentiary. The escaped convicts are soon placed on the FBI's Most Wanted list.

December 1942: FBI agents capture **Roger Touhy** at a boardinghouse in Chicago.

1943: American Communist Party member **Julius Rosenberg** is recruited by KGB agent Aleksander Feklisov to spy for the Soviet Union.

March 4, 1944: Murder, Inc., chief **Louis Lepke** is executed in the electric chair at Sing Sing prison.

1945: Meyer Lansky and **Bugsy Siegel** begin to establish a gambling hotel in a small western town called Las Vegas, Nevada.

June 1945: Julius Rosenberg arranges for his brother-in-law, David Greenglass, to provide a courier with classified information about the A-bomb.

December 1946: At a gangster summit in Havana, Cuba, **Bugsy Siegel** swears to fellow syndicate members that he has not stolen mob money through his Las Vegas gambling operation.

January 25, 1947: Retired gangster **Al Capone** dies at his mansion in Palm Island, Florida.

June 20, 1947: Bugsy Siegel is shot to death in the living room of **Virginia Hill**'s Beverly Hills mansion.

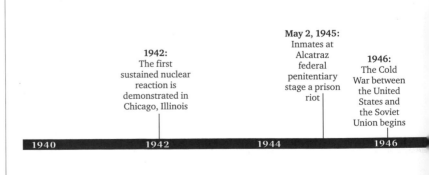

1942:
The first sustained nuclear reaction is demonstrated in Chicago, Illinois

May 2, 1945:
Inmates at Alcatraz federal penitentiary stage a prison riot

1946:
The Cold War between the United States and the Soviet Union begins

1940   1942   1944   1946

1949: Lloyd Barker, the only surviving member of the Barker Gang, is shot to death by his wife.

January 1949: Charles Ponzi dies in the charity ward of a Brazilian hospital at the age of sixty-six.

1950s: Working under **Sam Giancana, Sam Battaglia** becomes chief of the Chicago Outfit's narcotics operations.

May 10, 1950: The Senate Special Committee to Investigate Organized Crime in Interstate Commerce, spearheaded by Senator Estes Kefauver, subpoenas the testimony of numerous gangsters in a year-long attempt to piece together an accurate picture of organized crime in America.

June 15, 1950: Questioned by the FBI, David Greenglass implicates his sister, **Ethel Rosenberg,** and her husband, **Julius,** in espionage.

May 1951: "Queen of the Mob" **Virginia Hill** appears as a key witness before the Kefauver Committee and shocks committee members with her candid responses.

March 6, 1951: Ethel and Julius Rosenberg are tried for conspiracy to commit espionage.

June 19, 1953: In spite of worldwide pleas for clemency, **Ethel and Julius Rosenberg** are electrocuted at Sing Sing prison.

1954: Bank robber and kidnapper **Machine Gun Kelly** suffers a fatal heart attack in Leavenworth prison.

June 23, 1954: A federal grand jury charges **Virginia Hill** with income tax evasion.

1956: Retired swindler **Joseph Weil** is called to testify before a Senate subcommittee, led by Senator Estes Kefauver, investigating juvenile delinquency.

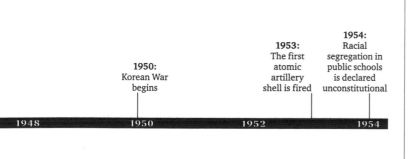

1950: Korean War begins

1953: The first atomic artillery shell is fired

1954: Racial segregation in public schools is declared unconstitutional

1948   1950   1952   1954

1957: Bugs Moran dies from cancer in Leavenworth penitentiary, where he is serving time for bank robbery.

October 25, 1957: Mobster Albert Anastasia is shot to death in the barber shop of the Park Sheraton Hotel in New York City. Rival gangsters **Carlo Gambino** and Vito Genovese are believed to be responsible for ordering the murder.

1959: FBI agents plant a microphone in the backroom of the Forest Park, Illinois, headquarters of mobster **Sam Giancana.**

November 25, 1959: Convicted kidnapper **Roger Touhy** is released from prison after the kidnapping he was found guilty of is revealed to have been a hoax.

December 17, 1959: Former bootlegger **Roger Touhy** is gunned down near his sister's Chicago home.

1960s: The U.S. government begins to subpoena gangster **Carlo Gambino** to appear before the grand jury to investigate his decades-long involvement in organized crime.

1965: After refusing to testify about the mob's activities before a federal grand jury in Chicago, mobster **Sam Giancana** is sentenced to one year in prison.

March 25, 1966: Virginia Hill dies from an overdose of sleeping pills near Salzburg, Austria.

December 1969: Diana Oughton, a former social activist, attends a secret meeting of the Weathermen, a terrorist organization, in Flint, Michigan.

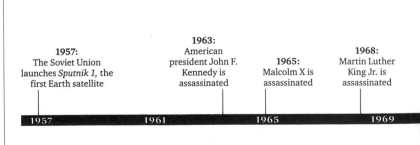

1957:
The Soviet Union launches *Sputnik 1,* the first Earth satellite

1963:
American president John F. Kennedy is assassinated

1965:
Malcolm X is assassinated

1968:
Martin Luther King Jr. is assassinated

1957   1961   1965   1969

1970: JoAnne Chesimard—also known as Assata Shakur—joins the Black Panther Party.

March 1970: Diana Oughton dies as a bomb explodes in a house in New York City. The house is a bomb factory for Weathermen terrorists.

March 23, 1971: Author **Clifford Irving** signs a contract with McGraw-Hill publishing company to write an authorized biography of billionaire Howard Hughes, who has not been interviewed by journalists since 1958.

November 1971: D. B. Cooper hijacks Northwest Airlines flight 305.

December 1971: Employees of **Jerry Schneider** inform officials at the Pacific Telephone & Telegraph company in Los Angeles, California, that their boss is using access to the phone company's computerized inventory system to order products illegally.

February 1972: Investigators for the Los Angeles District Attorney obtain a search warrant for the business of **Jerry Schneider.** Schneider is later charged with receiving stolen property and sentenced to two months in prison.

March 9, 1972: Author **Clifford Irving** is charged with federal conspiracy to defraud, forgery, and several other charges for writing the fake autobiography of Howard Hughes.

1973: Mobster **Sam Battaglia** dies in prison, having served six years of a fifteen-year sentence for extortion.

February 18, 1973: Retired mobster **Frank Costello** dies of natural causes at the age of eighty-two.

July 4, 1973: "To my people"—a speech in which **JoAnne Chesimard** describes herself as a black revolutionary—is publicly broadcast.

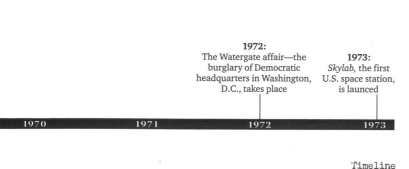

1972:
The Watergate affair—the burglary of Democratic headquarters in Washington, D.C., takes place

1973:
Skylab, the first U.S. space station, is launched

1970   1971   1972   1973

1974: JoAnne Chesimard and fellow Black Liberation Army member Fred Hilton are tried and acquitted of a 1972 bank robbery in New York.

February 4, 1974: Newspaper heiress **Patty Hearst** is kidnapped by members of the Symbionese Liberation Army (SLA).

April 5, 1974: Patty Hearst records a message to announce publicly that she has joined the SLA.

July 29, 1974: College dropout **Christopher Boyce** begins work at TRW Systems, an aerospace firm that works on many classified military programs. The following year Boyce and friend **Andrew Daulton Lee** devise a plan to provide Soviet agents with top-secret information.

June 2, 1975: John Gotti pleads guilty to attempted manslaughter in the second degree for the murder of James McBratney in Staten Island, New York.

September 18, 1975: Patty Hearst is captured with terrorist Wendy Yoshimura in an apartment in San Francisco.

October 15, 1975: Mobster **Carlo Gambino** dies of a heart attack at his home in Long Island, New York, at the age of seventy-three.

October 10, 1976: Convicted telephone thief **Jerry Schneider** appears on a *60 Minutes* television segment called "Dial E for Embezzlement."

1977: Gordon Kahl, a member of the conservative survivalist group called Posse Comitatus, is convicted of failing to file federal income tax returns. He is placed on probation.

March 25, 1977: JoAnne Chesimard is convicted of the murder of a New Jersey state trooper. She is sentenced to life in prison plus more than twenty-five years.

April 1977: Christopher Boyce and Andrew Daulton Lee— the Falcon and the Snowman—are tried for espionage. Both are convicted.

1974:
Richard M. Nixon resigns the U.S. presidency

1975:
The joint U.S.-Russian Apollo-Soyuz space mission begins

1977:
The neutron bomb is developed in the U.S.

1974   1975   1976   1977

November 5, 1978: FBI agents arrest computer thief **Stanley Rifkin** in Carlsbad, California.

January 1979: President Jimmy Carter commutes the prison sentence of convicted bank robber **Patty Hearst.**

February 13, 1979: Released on bail, computer thief **Stanley Rifkin** is arrested for initiating a wire fraud of the Union Bank of Los Angeles. A month later he is convicted of two counts of wire fraud and is sentenced to eight years in federal prison.

November 2, 1979: Convicted murderer **JoAnne Chesimard** escapes from the New Jersey Corrections Institute for women. She later flees to Cuba.

January 1980: Convicted spy **Christopher Boyce** escapes from a federal prison in Lompoc, California. Nineteen months later he is captured and returned to prison—with ninety years added to his original sentence.

April 1980: Two children discover a package containing several dozen $20 bills near Portland, Oregon. The serial numbers are traced to the ransom payment in the **D. B. Cooper** hijacking.

May 28, 1980: John Favara, the man responsible for the accidental killing of gangster **John Gotti**'s twelve-year-old son, disappears. He is never seen again.

January 15, 1983: **Meyer Lansky** dies of cancer in a New York hospital at the age of eighty-one.

February 13, 1983: Federal marshals attempt to serve tax evader **Gordon Kahl** with a warrant for violating parole. A shootout follows, in which two marshals are killed.

May 11, 1983: **Gordon Kahl** and two others are charged with the murders of two federal marshals.

June 4, 1983: **Gordon Kahl** dies in a shootout with federal marshals near Smithville, Arkansas.

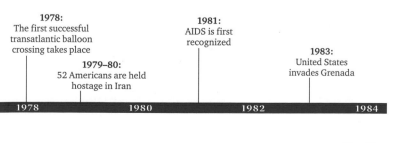

1978:
The first successful transatlantic balloon crossing takes place

1979–80:
52 Americans are held hostage in Iran

1981:
AIDS is first recognized

1983:
United States invades Grenada

1978   1980   1982   1984

April 1985: CIA agent **Aldrich Ames** begins to work as a Soviet spy.

June 2, 1986: San Francisco peace activist **Katya Komisaruk** destroys a government computer on the Vandenberg Air Force base as an anti-nuclear protest.

August 1986: Astronomer Clifford Stoll discovers a seventy-five cent shortfall in his computer system's accounting records. He later discovers that the shortfall is due to an unauthorized user who has broken into the system to access classified information without being traced.

March 13, 1987: Gangster **John Gotti** is tried on charges of racketeering. The "Teflon don" is acquitted.

November 1987: **Katya Komisaruk** is tried on one count of destruction of government property. During her trial, many supporters appear in court carrying white roses as a symbol of solidarity.

January 11, 1988: Convicted of destroying government property, **Katya Komisaruk** is sentenced to five years in federal prison.

March 2, 1989: Clifford Stoll's investigation of computer records leads to a spy ring of West German computer hackers. **Marcus Hess** and two others are arrested in Hanover, West Germany.

July 1989: Computer hacker **Kevin Mitnick** is sentenced to one year in federal prison at Lompoc, California, for breaking into telephone company computers and stealing long-distance access codes.

1992: John Gotti is tried and convicted of fourteen counts of racketeering and murder after being betrayed by former aide Salvatore "Sammy the Bull" Gravano.

May 12, 1993: The FBI begins a criminal investigation of **Aldrich Ames,** who is suspected of spying for the Soviets.

1989:
The Berlin Wall is destroyed

1990:
Persian Gulf War begins

1992:
Los Angeles riots

1986   1988   1990   1992

February 21, 1994: Soviet spy **Aldrich Ames** is arrested as he drives to work at CIA headquarters. He is later convicted of espionage and sentenced to life in prison.

December 24, 1994: Convicted hacker **Kevin Mitnick** steals data from the home computer of computer security expert Tsutomu Shimomura.

February 15, 1995: Federal agents arrest **Kevin Mitnick** in Raleigh, North Carolina, without a struggle.

April 19, 1995: A bomb explodes in front of the Alfred P. Murrah Federal Building in Oklahoma City, Oklahoma, killing 168 people. **Timothy McVeigh** is arrested a short time later.

November 21, 1996: Archaeologists find what they believe to be the long-lost flagship of **Blackbeard** the pirate.

April 1997: The trial of suspected terrorist **Timothy McVeigh** begins in Denver, Colorado.

June 2, 1997: **Timothy McVeigh** is convicted of all eleven charges against him involving the Oklahoma City bombing.

December 1997: A group of hackers break into an Internet site and leave behind a computerized ransom note threatening to release a computer virus if **Kevin Mitnick** is not set free.

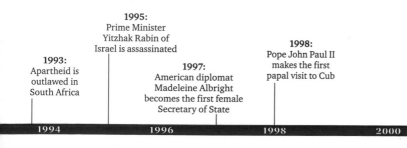

1993:
Apartheid is outlawed in South Africa

1995:
Prime Minister Yitzhak Rabin of Israel is assassinated

1997:
American diplomat Madeleine Albright becomes the first female Secretary of State

1998:
Pope John Paul II makes the first papal visit to Cub

1994 1996 1998 2000

Picture Credits

The photographs and illustrations appearing in *Outlaws, Mobsters & Crooks: From the Old West to the Internet* were received from the following sources:

On the cover: Al Capone (**Archive Photos, Inc. Reproduced by permission**).

AP/Wide World Photos, Inc. Reproduced by permission: pp. 3, 11, 18, 31, 35, 45, 50, 56, 67, 72, 80, 87, 100, 109, 110, 127, 139, 151, 156, 159, 178, 186, 190, 193, 207, 217, 220, 226, 227, 230, 241, 247, 262, 266, 269, 270, 283, 305, 310, 311, 313, 328, 336, 351, 373, 392, 394, 437, 440, 443, 451, 459, 462; **Archive Photos, Inc. Reproduced by permission:** pp. 13, 21, 89, 121, 235, 292, 378, 410, 450; **UPI/Corbis-Bettmann. Reproduced by permission:** pp. 16, 22, 28, 41, 47, 54, 55, 58, 75, 93, 96, 105, 144, 147, 164, 177, 205, 261, 278, 294, 297, 325, 430, 434, 448, 456, 465; **Photograph by Greta Pratt. New York Times Co./Archive Photos, Inc. Reproduced by permission:** p. 39; **The Granger Collection, New York. Reproduced by permission:** pp. 113, 333, 355, 367, 387, 397, 412, 419, 492; **Popperfoto/Archive Photos, Inc. Reproduced by permission:** p. 133; **Photograph by Tammy Lechner. Los Angeles Times Photo. Reproduced by permission:** p. 189; **Reuters/The News and Observer-Jim/Archive Photos, Inc. Reproduced by permission:** p. 197; **Reuters/Corbis-Bettmann. Reproduced by permission:** p. 221; **Wyoming Division of Cultural Resources. Reproduced by permission:** p. 253; **Reuters/Jim Bourg/Archive Photos. Reproduced by permission:** p. 315; **Photograph by Eric Draper. AP/Wide World Photos, Inc. Reproduced by permission:** p. 317; **American Stock/Archive Photos, Inc. Reproduced by permission:** pp. 341, 347, 368; **The Library of Congress:** p. 360; **Corbis-Bettmann. Reproduced by permission:** pp. 364, 384, 398, 486, 490; **Corbis. Reproduced by permission:** pp. 380, 477, 482.

Computer Criminals

In 1823, English visionary Charles Babbage (1792–1871) persuaded the British government to finance an "analytical engine." This would have been a machine that could undertake any kind of calculation. It would have been driven by steam, and the program of operations would have been stored on a punched tape. The system was not completed. Although he never built a working computer, Babbage thought out many of the basic principles that guide many computers today.

But chances are he never envisioned the criminal possibilities that the computer age provides. Stolen secrets and data theft. Unauthorized wire transfers. Illegal access to phone company products and services. The computer age provides unprecedented opportunities for far reaching criminal applications. Some of the computer criminals you'll read about in this chapter were interested primarily in proving what they were capable of. Others used their skills for personal gain—and even to spy for a foreign government. And in most cases, the investigations that led to their capture offer a fascinating look at a high tech game of cat and mouse.

Marcus Hess

Active: 1986-1989

*Between 1986 and 1989—at a time when computer security was an unexplored field—
a West German named Marcus Hess and a number of other computer hackers took
advantage of loopholes in computer systems to gain unauthorized access to sensitive
information. Pioneers in computer espionage, they reportedly sold that information to
Soviet officials.*

A RECIPE FOR CHAOS

In the late 1980s Marcus Hess worked as a computer programmer for a small computer company in West Germany. He
also belonged to a computer group known as the Chaos Computer Club, based in Hamburg, West Germany. As a member of
Chaos, Hess and a number of other West German hackers
became involved in a computer-based espionage ring. Hess—
who was known as "the Hanover Hacker" (because he lived in
Hanover, West Germany)—started with a telephone call from
his home phone. By making a local computer modem call in
Hanover, he tapped into a European data network called Datex.
From there he entered a library computer at the University of
Bremen in West Germany. Tampering with the system's software, he fooled the computer into thinking that he was an
authorized user with special privileges. Through the Bremen
account, he connected to the Tymnet network in the United
States. From there, he entered a computer at Lawrence Berkeley
Laboratories in California that gave him access to other systems
across the country.

The cyber hound who hunted the "Hanover Hacker"

A scientist by training, Clifford Stoll viewed the pursuit of a hacker as an interesting "problem." At a time when computer security was an unexplored field, he discovered a trail that indicated that the hacker was reading—and copying—extremely sensitive information concerning national security.

"I wasn't interested in the hackers," Stoll later reported in *Compute* magazine. "To come across people who believe that it's their right or responsibility to break into computers doesn't interest me at all. I'm a physicist. I do science. It struck me as more interesting technically—[I began wondering] what's happening? What's the connectivity here? What's permitting this? Here is a field of study no one has worked on before: how do insecure networks, through holes in security, allow exploitation of databases in a way that nobody's ever talked about before?"

Small change

In 1986, Stoll, who held a Ph.D. in astronomy, had a job designing software for the Keck Observatory in Berkeley, California. But when the project's grant money ran out in August of that year, he was transferred to another job—managing computers in the same building. On the second day of his new job at Lawrence Berkeley Laboratories, Stoll received a simple assignment. He was to find out why the computer's accounting system showed a seventy-five cent deficit (shortage).

First, Stoll examined the computer's accounting programs to find out whether the software was responsible for the billing error. He found nothing wrong with the program—but he did find something suspicious. An unfamiliar user named Hunter had logged onto the system briefly—just long enough to use seventy-five cents worth of time. Since the computer center had no record of Hunter, Stoll erased the account from the system.

A hacker in their midst

But the mystery did not end there. Next Stoll received a report from the National Computer Security Center, a unit of the National Security Agency (NSA). Someone from Lawrence Berkeley Laboratory had attempted to break into an NSA computer system in Fort Meade, Maryland. After looking into the incident, Stoll discovered that the break-in attempt had originated from the account of someone named Joe Sventek. But

AN APPETITE FOR MILITARY DATA

Hess operated like a burglar who goes from one house to another attempting to find an unlocked door. In all, he tried to

Sventek was not in Berkeley at the time of the break-in: he was in England.

At first, Stoll suspected that a student at the nearby University of California was attempting to hack his way into NSA computers—using an account at Lawrence Berkeley Laboratory—to pull an elaborate prank. To find the culprit, he created a monitoring station that allowed him to trace the intruder's online movements.

Looking at a spy

Stoll set up programs that were able to determine every time the hacker entered the Berkeley computer. When he was not in the computer laboratory, he wore a pocket pager that alerted him when the hacker was online. Stoll programmed the computers in his surveillance station to monitor and record every keystroke the intruder made—without the intruder's knowledge.

What he found led him to believe that the hacker was not local—nor was he a novice (inexperienced beginner). The hacker communicated over a worldwide network and had created a program that acted as a master key to unlock protected files—which allowed him to gain entry into hundreds of other computer systems on the networks the Lawrence Berkeley Lab employed, including academic, industrial, and military computers.

Little help from the feds

Because the hacker was secretly gaining access to sensitive documents, Stoll felt it was his duty to inform the government organizations of the intruder's activities. At first he encountered resistance. "When we first took it to the FBI, they laughed at us," he told *Science* magazine. FBI agents claimed that they could not become involved unless classified information had been stolen or more than $500,000 in computer resources had been lost. All Stoll could produce was the seventy-five cent shortfall. A scientist at the National Computer Security Center informed him that it was the agency's job to design computers that are theoretically secure—not to help out those who had already experienced hacker attacks.

Acting on a suggestion from his girlfriend (and later wife), Martha Matthews, Stoll managed to bait the hacker into revealing his home base. Stoll's investigative work ultimately led to the arrest of Marcus Hess and other members of the Computer Chaos Club. Later offered jobs as a computer-security specialist at the CIA and elsewhere, Stoll turned them down to return to his first love, astronomy. He accepted a job as an astronomer at Harvard's Smithsonian Observatory in Cambridge, Massachusetts.

enter about four hundred and fifty computers—of which he was able to enter approximately thirty. Much of Hess's activity involved the Milnet—a computer network that involves defense contractors and military installations. Administered by the Penta-

Clifford Stoll,
astronomer and spy
tracker.

gon, the Milnet contains vast quantities of sensitive information. Hess's many targets included computers at an Air Force space division in El Segundo, California; army bases in Alabama and Georgia; the Buckner Army Base in Okinawa, Japan; the Mitre Corporation, a Virginia defense contractor; the Navy Coastal Systems command in Panama City, Florida, and others.

Once he hacked his way into a computer system, Hess was very deliberate and methodical in his attack. To look for sensitive information about military, nuclear, and space research projects in the United States and elsewhere, he used keywords such as "nuclear" and "SDI" to search documents. (SDI stands for "Strategic Defense Initiative"—a defense program also known as "Star Wars.") Hess located information on intelligence satellites, semiconductor design research, space shuttle missions, navy missiles, and plans for chemical warfare. He also examined systems he entered for passwords to other computers.

A TRAP IS SET

Hess's interest in military information is ultimately what led investigators to his doorstep. Clifford Stoll, an astronomer who tracked Hess's movements for eighteen months, decided to lay a trap to entice the hacker to stay online long enough for the origin of the modem call to be traced. Stoll planted phony national security files that supposedly contained information on the Strategic Defense Initiative in the Lawrence Berkeley computer. The file was called "SDI Network Project."

Hess took the bait. Intrigued by the information he saw, he downloaded the file to his home computer. The process took more than one hour—more than enough time for authorities to trace the call. West German police, working with the FBI, were able to trace the hacker's call to an apartment in Hanover—at #3A Glocksee Strasse. On March 2, 1989, Marcus Hess was arrested at the apartment. The West German police also seized Hess's computer, records of computer passwords, and computer logs that contained the protocols (first draft) of a much-publicized, July 27, 1987 invasion of a National Aeronautics and Space Administration (NASA) computer.

Hess and two other West Germans, Peter Carl and Kirk-Otto Brezinski, who were also reportedly members of the Chaos Computer Club, were formally charged with selling software, military computer passwords, and other sensitive data to the KGB—the Soviet intelligence agency. In all, eight young men were suspected of selling secrets to the Soviets.

United States officials turned the matter over to German authorities. As far as U.S. government officials could determine, the hackers had not provided the Soviets with information that seriously compromised the nation's security. German authorities eventually released Hess because they did not have enough evidence to hold him. Jim Christy, the assistant chief of computer crime at the U.S. Air Force Office of Special Investigations in Washington, D.C., later charged that Hess's attorney had used a little-known loophole in the legal system. The loophole prevented the government from looking at important files that were contained on Hess's computer—files which might have provided ammunition for his prosecution.

Who **are** you gonna call?

Why did Clifford Stoll, an astronomer, become involved in an eighteen-month investigation tracking a computer spy? He later explained, "I was walking along one of the basement corridors and I happened to glance up. The open ceiling was brimming with wires, pipes, and cables. Most of them were clearly marked: hot water, cold water, waste water, gas, steam, electric conduit. And then I saw a bright orange Ethernet cable [a cable over which computers communicate in a local area network]. It was unlabeled but I knew what it was. And then it struck me. If the Ethernet cable broke, there'd be a puddle of bits and bytes on the floor and who would I call? If someone was stealing electricity, we had an electrician. If someone was purloining [stealing] water, there was a plumber on staff. But who is responsible for protecting the Lab's information, which is far more valuable commodity than electricity or water? It came into my head that I was responsible."

Sources for Further Reading

Elmer-DeWitt, Phillip. "A Bold Raid on Computer Security." *Time* (May 2, 1988), p. 58.

Hoffman, Russell D. *High Tech Today*. [Online] Available http://www.animatedsoftware.com/hightech/cliffsto.htm, December 11, 1997.

Kunen, James S. "Astronomer Cliff Stoll Stars In the Espionage Game, But For Him Spying Doesn't Really Compute." *People Weekly* (December 11, 1989), pp. 118–120.

Lehmann-Haupt, Christopher. "On the Electronic Trail of a Computer Spy." *The New York Times* (October 19, 1989), p. C23.

Marshall, Eliot. "German Spy Ring Broken." *Science* (March 24, 1989), p. 1545.

McCartney, Robert J. "West German Charged with Espionage In Computer Intrusion Investigation." *The Washington Post* (March 4, 1989), p. A16.

Mckeeman, Darren P. "Cliff Stoll Tells All." *Compute* (January 1992), p. 144.

Richards, Evelyn. "Computer Detective Followed Trail to Hacker Spy Suspect; Work Called Key to West German's Arrest." *The Washington Post* (March 4, 1989), p. A1.

"West Germany Arrests Computer Hackers." *Facts on File World News Digest* (March 10, 1989), p. 157F3.

Katya Komisaruk
(Susan Alexis Komisaruk)
Born: 1958

As an anti-nuclear protest, Komisaruk destroyed a government computer—a crime for which she later said she expected to go to court. In committing a crime for which she intended to be caught and punished, she hoped to bring the anti-nuclear cause into the public eye and help steer the United States away from nuclear war.

RADICAL BEGINNINGS

Born in the late 1950s, Susan Alexis Komisaruk was raised in Michigan and California. Her parents, a psychiatrist and homemaker who later divorced, were well-educated liberals who taught their daughter to question authority. Born to a Jewish family with roots in the Ukraine, Komisaruk had relatives who died in the Holocaust (the period of persecution and extermination of European Jews by Nazi Germany). Her parents, who were Zionists, instilled in their daughter a sharp awareness of the Holocaust and of the events that led up to it. (Zionism is a movement interested in recovering for Jewish people the historic Palestinian homeland.)

An intelligent young woman, Komisaruk—who received the nickname "Katya" as a child—became bored with high school after just one year. She quit high school at the age of sixteen and attended Mills College in California. One year later, she transferred to Reed College in Oregon, where she majored in the classics—the study of Greek and Latin literature. In 1978, when she was just nineteen years old, she graduated from college.

Vandenberg Air Force Base in California, where Komisaruk broke in to destroy a computer.

Next, Komisaruk enrolled in the business school at the University of California at Berkeley. The experience transformed her. Raised by parents who were not politically active, Komisaruk found herself becoming increasingly politicized. Early in her first term as a business student, she became convinced that American business is part of a corrupt system that exploits (makes unethical use of) workers and destroys the environment.

She also concluded that politics were unduly affected by money, and that military spending was destroying the nation's economy.

CIVIL DISOBEDIENCE

Komisaruk later told the *Los Angeles Times,* "All of this left me extremely politicized. It came to me I had to do something. I felt I should go to a rally and protest." And protest she did. In 1982, she joined a demonstration at Lawrence Livermore Laboratories. Although she was arrested and detained for two days, the experience left her convinced of the power of activism.

After graduating from the University of California with a master's degree in business administration, Komisaruk worked as an administrator at the Graduate Theological Union in Berkeley, California. She lived with other activists and contributed half of the money she earned to the cause. She became increasingly involved in a number of issues—especially those involving anti-nuclear activities. She also helped establish the Community Defense, Inc., an organization that was established to provide legal assistance to people involved in civil disobedience—or nonviolent protests.

After one year, Komisaruk quit her job at the Graduate Theological Union. She worked at part-time jobs and continued to organize and participate in anti-nuclear activities. In 1983, she was arrested for taking part in a protest movement at Vandenberg Air Force Base in California. Komisaruk spent a short period in jail for her role in attempting to prevent the launching of an MX missile at Vandenberg.

THE VANDENBERG INCIDENT

As Komisaruk became more involved in anti-nuclear activities, so did her conviction that her activism would eventually result in long-term imprisonment. On June 2, 1986, she

The margin of error

Komisaruk believed that she was destroying a computer whose global positioning system provided the U.S. with first-strike superiority over the Soviet Union. But the U.S. government claimed that the computer was no longer in use and was being stored as surplus. What is more, government officials claimed that the satellite navigation system had been moved to Colorado more than one year earlier. Further, Pentagon officials announced that any claims that the NAVSTAR system was intended to provide first-strike capability are "flatly wrong." Assistant U.S. Attorney Nora Manella, who prosecuted the case, claimed that Komisaruk was misinformed. She told reporters, "We have here a woman whose zeal exceeded her level of knowledge by a wide margin."

Flowers, cookies, and a poem

Komisaruk visited the Vandenberg Air Force Base armed with tools with which she planned to destroy a government computer. She also carried a bag of cookies, a bouquet of flowers, and a poem—as gifts for soldiers she might encounter. She was afraid that well-armed soldiers who discovered her on the base without permission in the middle of the night might shoot first and ask questions later. Komisaruk's poem read,

> I have no gun
>
> You must have lots.
>
> Let's not be hasty
>
> No cheap shots.
>
> Please have a cookie and a nice day.

Komisaruk later explained why she had left behind such an odd assortment of items. "I was afraid," she said, "that the guards would respond to an alarm—that there might be these soldiers dashing in with their automatic weapons, and it would be like Kent State [on May 4 1970, four Kent State University students were shot and killed by national guardsmen during an anti-war protest], where young panicky men who had been through boot camp and had a lot of brainwashing were suddenly faced with an emergency and did what they were trained to do, which was pull the trigger. I didn't want to be the target. I thought one way to get around that was to have them come across the flowers, poem, and cookies first, anything to distract them and make them stop and think for a few minutes before they went swarming in there." Komisaruk never faced any soldiers during her two-hour visit to Vandenberg.

returned to Vandenberg Air Force Base by a back-road route—armed with a hammer, crowbar, cordless drill, and bolt cutters—aware that the action she was about to take would probably earn her an extended prison sentence.

Komisaruk's target was a sophisticated Air Force navigation computer housed in a building on the base. She believed that the computer's NAVSTAR global positioning system, which had the ability to locate Soviet missile silos (underground shelters for missiles), was intended to give the U.S. "first-strike" nuclear capability. By destroying the computer, she intended to prevent the U.S. government from mounting a first-strike attack against the Soviet Union. In short, she believed she was acting to prevent the possibility of nuclear war.

Komisaruk walked onto the Air Force base in the middle of the night. Although the compound was surrounded by a barbed wire fence, the gate stood wide open. She entered through the open gate, closed it from the inside—and then locked it with a bicycle lock she had brought with her. She also squeezed epoxy (a type of glue) into the lock to make it more difficult for security personnel to enter. She placed a bouquet of flowers, cookies, and poem at the gate to evoke compassion from guards who might try to stop her.

After breaking into a building that contained the navigation computer, she went to work. Using the tools she brought with her, she hammered and pried at the valuable computer. She later reported that she was terrified throughout the experience: "I was afraid; I'd never done anything like this before. At any minute, I expected to be caught; my stomach was churning, and I had to run into the bushes more than once."

Two hours later, the twenty-eight- year- old activist walked off the base, leaving behind a wrecked computer and satellite dish. The computer chips were piled on the floor, where Komisaruk had done a dance over them. Next, she hitchhiked back to the San Francisco area, where she consulted with lawyers. The following day a press release appeared. It said: "Peace activist destroys satellite control center, gives self up, press conference noon Wednesday, San Francisco Federal building." At the news conference, Komisaruk told reporters, "You're a party to mass murder if you don't get out there and try to stop it." Further, she defended her actions under international law—such as the Nuremberg Treaty, signed by the United States. Under the treaty, nations agree never to prepare for or initiate a war of aggression. Komisaruk admitted to destroying the government computer, and surrendered to authorities.

Komisaruk's lead defense attorney, Leonard Weinglass.

TRIAL STRATEGIES

Komisaruk was arrested and charged with two crimes: destruction of government property and sabotage (a deliberate effort to harm an endeavor). She was tried in November 1987. Her defense team was made up of Leonard Weinglass, a respect-

The White Rose

Komisaruk called the Vandenberg Air Force Base incident the "White Rose Action." The name was inspired by a group of young German activists known as "The White Rose" about whom Komisaruk had learned when she was fourteen years old. Active during World War II (1939–1945), the Christian members of the White Rose group urged their countrymen not to participate in the Nazi persecution of Jews. In 1943, the protesters were arrested and executed.

During Komisaruk's trial, her supporters in the court room held white roses to demonstrate their solidarity (unity). They also distributed the following statement at a pre-trial press conference: "During the Third Reich [Germany's Nazi era] a small group of gentile [Christian] students, calling themselves 'The White Rose,' chose to resist [Adolf] Hitler. They tried to tell their fellow citizens what horrors were being committed in their name."

ed New York civil rights attorney, Dan Williams, William Simpich, and others. Komisaruk's defense relied on international law that prevents the U.S. from planning a war of aggression—such as a first-strike nuclear attack against the Soviet Union. The government filed a motion to limit Komisaruk's defense. Government attorneys argued that Komisaruk's motives should not enter into the trial—and the computer's purpose should not be taken into consideration.

Federal district judge William J. Rea approved the government's motion. Defense attorneys were not allowed to argue that Komisaruk was justified under international law that prevents nations from planning or launching wars of aggression. That is, Komisaruk's attorneys could not claim that their client was acting to prevent a crime of nuclear aggression—a crime against humanity. One day before the trial started, prosecuting attorneys dropped the count of sabotage, which involves the "willful destruction with intent." In order to prove intent, the government needed to examine Komisaruk's motive for destroying the computer—something prosecuting attorneys did not want discussed at the trial. All that remained to be settled at trial was the question of whether Komisaruk had destroyed the government computer.

A HARSH SENTENCE

Komisaruk's trial lasted just four days. After less than two hours' deliberation, the federal court jury found Komisaruk guilty of one count of destroying government property. Soon after the verdict was announced, security guards forcibly removed several of Komisaruk's supporters from the courtroom because they created a disturbance by attempting to make speeches. The guilty verdict carried a maximum sentence of ten years in prison. (If Komisaruk had been found guilty of the additional charge of sabotage, she could have faced another ten years' imprisonment.) Major General Donald O. Aldridge, the commanding officer of Vandenberg Air Force Base, sent a letter to the court urging the judge to issue a harsh sentence to discourage other activists from taking similar steps.

Aware that she was about the be sentenced to a long imprisonment, Komisaruk decided to inform Judge Rea of her opinion of the trial. She said:

> I'm in a delicate position. I believe I am expected to plead for understanding, for mercy . . . and the stakes are very high. What does one say to ward off the nightmare of ten years in prison? . . . I don't think we can have an honest dialogue, because I stand here below your platform and I'm afraid of you . . . and my stomach hurts and my mouth is dry and my heart is pounding and I wish I were anywhere but your courtroom. Yet there's one thing that bothers me more than my fear of what punishment you're going to pronounce. And that's the fact that I made a coward's choice during my trial. Like the sycophants [someone who flatters important people] who assured their naked emperor that he was beautifully dressed, I pretended that the trial was a fair and just proceeding. I was so intimidated [frightened] by this huge courtroom, by all the marshals and officials, by the formal language and ceremony, and by you, Your Honor, that I failed to speak the truth. I never really stated just how ludicrous [laughable] the proceeding was. . . . Your robes and bench are transparent, Your Honor. They cannot cover up injustice. They only hide it for a while.

On January 11, 1988, Judge Rea sentenced Komisaruk to five years in federal prison. He also ordered her to pay

An unfair trial?

Tried for destroying government property, Komisaruk was not allowed to appeal to international law to defend her actions. Her attorneys believed that the court's decision was unfair—and presented jurors with a one-sided version of the incident. Komisaruk's lead attorney, Leonard Weinglass, later complained, "We didn't get a right to have a jury trial in this case. We got a right to be present when the government presented its case to twelve people."

The making of a martyr

Komisaruk's attorney argued that his client's stiff sentence would not discourage other activists from similar acts of disobedience. He told reporters, "They have succeeded in making a martyr, not in deterring anyone.'

Nuclear holocaust

"When my mother was young, her worst nightmare was that the Nazis would come," Komisaruk once explained. "Mine was the flash of light signaling the explosion of a nuclear bomb. I am Jewish, and for a long time, I worried that anti-Semitism [hostility toward Jews] could again become a destructive force. Later, I feared that we Americans could be the ones to unleash a holocaust [total destruction—such as Nazi Germany's attempt to destroy European Jews], this time nuclear."

$500,000 in restitution (to make good for a loss)—the estimated replacement cost of the computer. Rea explained the harsh sentence as something intended "to pass the word along that you can't do these things and get a slap on the wrist." Dozens of Komisaruk's supporters were present at the sentencing—many of whom cried when the sentence was announced.

THE JUDGE RESPONDS

After Komisaruk's sentencing, Judge Rea announced, "[Komisaruk] says she has obeyed a higher law. Well, if every person in this country could take [the law] into his or her hands . . . we would have a society of anarchy [choas]. We cannot permit you and others motivated as you are to destroy taxpayers' property merely because you feel that what is going on in this country is not to your liking."

Sources for Further Reading

Davis, Cheryl A. "Five Years for the 'White Rose.'" *Progressive* (March 1988), pp. 14–15.

Hendrix, Kathleen. "Katya Komisaruk's Revolution: Why a Berkeley MBA Trashed a Multimillion-Dollar Air Force Computer in the Name of Peace." *Los Angeles Times* (November 11, 1987), View section, p. 1.

Murphy, Kim. "Anti-War Activist Gets Five Years for Junking Computer." *Los Angeles Times* (January 12, 1988), p. 1.

Murphy, Kim. "'Higher Law' Behind Attack on Computer, Activist Says." *Los Angeles Times* (November 14, 1987), p. 32.

Murphy, Kim. "Peace Activist Guilty of Wrecking Computer." *Los Angeles Times* (November 17, 1987), Metro section, p. 1.

Murphy, Kim. "Woman Who Destroyed Computer Denied Anti-Nuclear Defense." *Los Angeles Times* (October 27, 1987), p. 25.

Kevin Mitnick

Born: 1965?

Kevin D. Mitnick made a name for himself by hacking his way into telephone networks and vandalizing corporate, government, and university computers. For a while, according to assistant United States attorney Kent Walker, "He was arguably the most wanted computer hacker in the world."

A YOUTHFUL PHONE PHREAK

Mitnick grew up in the San Fernando Valley near Los Angeles, California. After his parents divorced when he was three years old, he lived with his mother, who worked long hours as a waitress at a delicatessen. As a youth he had few friends. He rarely saw his father and grew up lonely and isolated.

While in his teens, Mitnick got into phone phreaking—using electronic techniques to gain illegal access to telephone services. He became friends with other phone phreaks and often hung out with a group that met at a Shakey's Pizza Parlor in Los Angeles to plot ways to break into local computer and communications systems. Together with other phone phreak friends—such as a young woman who called herself Susan Thunder and a young man who went by the name of Roscoe—he searched the dumpsters behind phone company offices for manuals that would provide vital information about company computers.

Mitnick first got into trouble with the law during his teens. As a student at Monroe High School in North Hills, California,

Susan Thunder

Mitnick met Susan Thunder as a teenager, when both were involved with a phone phreaking group in Los Angeles. (Susan Thunder was the young woman's online name.) Thunder dropped out of school in the eighth grade, worked as a prostitute in Hollywood, and later got into phone phreaking and computer hacking. In 1982, she testified in a case that landed the seventeen-year-old Mitnick on probation for stealing computer manuals from the Pacific Bell Telephone Company. She also described to a U.S. Senate Subcommittee how she and other phone phreaks had used their personal computers to change their victims' credit ratings—and replace them with obscenities. What's more, she claimed the group had attempted to shut down the telephone system in all of California. After a brief period in Las Vegas, Nevada, as a professional poker player, Thunder returned to California. In 1994, she was elected city clerk in a small town in the desert.

he broke into the computer system of the Los Angeles Unified School District. He could have changed students' grades, but he did not. He also reportedly hacked his way into the military's North American Air Defense Command computers in Colorado just for fun. When Mitnick, just seventeen years old, was caught stealing valuable technical manuals from the Pacific Bell Telephone Company, a judge sentenced him to probation (a trial period to test his good behavior). In spite of his brush with the law, Mitnick returned to hacking. After he was caught breaking into computers at a local university, he was sentenced to six months in jail.

Public servants

Hackers rely on flaws in computer systems to gain access to off-limits information. Many hackers believe that by bringing these flaws to light, they are performing a sort of public service.

A COMPUTER ADDICT

When Mitnick was twenty-three, he met Bonnie Vitello, who worked for the phone company. A short while later, Mitnick and Vitello were married. Mitnick's computer hacking created a strain on the relationship, and the couple eventually divorced.

Mitnick attracted the attention of security experts in December 1988, when he was charged with breaking into MCI telephone computers and stealing long-distance codes. By secretly reading the electronic mail of security officials at MCI and Digital Equipment Corporation, Mitnick discovered how the companies' computers and phone equipment were protected against hackers. In July 1989, he was convicted and sentenced to one year in federal prison at Lompoc, California—followed by a period at a rehabilitation center. One of Mitnick's defense attorneys had managed to convince the judge that his client was "addicted" to computers—and that, like an alcoholic, he was not able to control his behavior.

Following his release from federal prison, Mitnick was sent to Gateways Beit T'Shuvah, a residential program designed to help addicts overcome their addictions. (The program's name is Hebrew for "house of repentance.") There he followed a Twelve-Step program modeled after Alcoholics Anonymous. He spent six months at the rehabilitation center—during which time he was forbidden to use a computer or a modem.

Mitnick was released early from Beit T'Shuvah, in the spring of 1990. One of the conditions of his parole specified that he was forbidden to use computers until he could demonstrate that he was able to control his behavior. Mitnick returned to Los Angeles in early 1992, following the drug-related death of his half-brother. He was employed for a while with his father, Alan, who was a general contractor. When that did not work out, he took a job with a private investigation agency called Tel Tec Investigations.

In September 1992, federal officials, armed with a search warrant, raided Mitnick's apartment. Mitnick, who was suspected of breaking into a Pacific Bell computer, was nowhere to be found. But coded disks and documents provided proof of his activities. In November, a federal judge issued a warrant for the hacker's arrest. Mitnick had violated the conditions of his parole. Aware that the heat was on, Mitnick went went into hiding.

MERRY CHRISTMAS, MR. SHIMOMURA

For more than two years, Mitnick managed to elude federal officials. But on Christmas Day 1994, he committed a fatal mistake. Mitnick broke into the home computer of Tsutomu Shimomura, a computational physicist who worked as a computer security expert at the Supercomputer Center in San Diego. Using a modem, Mitnick "spoofed" his way into Shimomura's networked databases. "Spoofing" involves fooling a computer into thinking that it is communicating with a friendly computer.

Cat meets mouse

When Mitnick finally met Tsutomu Shimomura, the man who led the FBI to his doorstep, he said, "Hello, Tsutomu. I respect your skills." Shimomura said nothing in reply. Later, when asked what he thought about Mitnick's remark, he told a *Newsweek* reporter, "You know, I feel sorry for him. But he's caused a lot of people a lot of grief, and his behavior is clearly unacceptable. I don't know what's wrong with him, but he keeps getting in trouble. Throwing him in prison isn't a very elegant solution, but I don't have a better idea."

Tsutomu Shimomura

Shimomura was born in Nagoya, Japan, on October 23, 1964. Both his father, Osamu, and mother, Akemi, were biochemists. In the 1960s, Shimomura and his younger sister, Sachi, moved to the United States with their parents. Osamu Shimomura took a position as a research faculty member at Princeton University in New Jersey.

Shimomura's parents taught him the value of experimentation. Describing his upbringing in the book *Takedown* (a record of his pursuit of Mitnick), he wrote: "From my first steps my family encouraged me to be curious. I was provoked to ask questions, to which I never received "because" replies. My parents' response was often to suggest an experiment through which I could determine for myself the answer."

An exceptionally bright student, Shimomura skipped several grades. He entered his first year of high school when he was just twelve years old. Bored with school, he dropped out before he graduated in order to work at the astrophysics department at Princeton University. Next, he enrolled at Caltech in Pasadena, California, as a physics major.

While still an undergraduate student, he received a call from a team of researchers at Los

Mitnick took over a computer that was "friendly" to the computer he wanted to enter. Once inside the target computer, he stole hundreds of documents and software programs that contained sensitive information about computer security. The attack lasted from 2 P.M. on Christmas Day until 6 P.M. the following evening.

Shimomura was on his way to Lake Tahoe, California, for a ski vacation, when he was informed that someone had broken into his databases. He returned home and immediately set out to discover the identity of the intruder. On December 27, he received a mocking message on his office voice mail. A man's computer-altered voice said: "My technique is the best. Damn you. I know sendmail technique. Don't you know who I am? Me and my friends, we'll kill you." Next, another voice said, "Hey, boss, my kung fu is really good." Before the end of the month, Shimomura had received another message: "Your technique will be defeated," the voice said. "Your technique is no good."

After Shimomura made the voice messages available on the Internet (in computer audio files), he received yet another mes-

Alamos National Laboratory in New Mexico. The team was building a specialized computer for physics research and they wanted to know if Shimomura was interested in working on the project. In 1984, Shimomura accepted a postdoctoral position at Los Alamos. He was just nineteen years old—and had not even graduated from high school.

By the time he was twenty-five, Shimomura was recruited to work at the San Diego Supercomputer Center, a federally funded operation. He gained a reputation as a brilliant, driven (and somewhat difficult) trouble-shooter. Having become an expert in computer security, Shimomura also worked as a consultant for the U.S. Air Force, the Federal Bureau of Investigation (FBI), the National Security Agency, and others.

After Kevin Mitnick broke into his computer on Christmas Day 1994, Shimomura relentlessly tracked the intruder's every move. For more than two years, Mitnick had managed to elude federal authorities. Seven weeks after Mitnick tangled with Shimomura's computer, the man who has been called the "Eliot Ness of the Internet" led FBI agents to the fugitive hacker's hideout. He later claimed that Mitnick's hacking involved nothing new or imaginative. Mitnick, he told reporters, "wasn't very hard to catch."

sage. This time, the computer-altered voice said, "Ah Tsutomu, my learned disciple. I see that you put my voice on the Net. I'm very disappointed my son." The messages provided little information about the intruder's identity. But they indicated that he viewed the situation as a game of wits.

THE HUNT FOR THE HACKER

For most of the following month, no new clues appeared. On January 27, 1995, Bruce Koball, a computer programmer, received notice from an online service called WELL. The notice informed him that his account was taking up too much disk space: Koball's account suddenly claimed hundreds of millions of bytes of storage space. But Koball had not been using his account. When he looked at the files in his account, he found Shimomura's name. The next day, when he read a newspaper story about the theft of files from a computer expert named Shimomura, he realized what had happened. The computer thief had stashed Shimomura's files in his account. And that was not all. The WELL account included secret codes for various companies, password files, and more than twenty-one thousand credit card numbers.

Shimomura and a few other computer experts formed a surveillance team at the WELL headquarters in Sausalito, California, in order to track the hacker's online movements. Using sophisticated programs, they were able to monitor every key-stroke the intruder made. By February 8, the team had determined that their subject was gaining access to WELL through Netcom, another Internet provider. The team of cyber-sleuths moved to Netcom's headquarters in San Jose, California. There, they monitored the intruder's modem calls. Using Shimomura's complicated security programs, they unraveled the tangled computer connections that allowed the hacker to connect to the Internet without being identified.

But the intruder's identity was slowly coming to light. Mitnick was already a well-known hacker—whose habits and interests were familiar to computer security experts such as Shimomura. Like Mitnick, the intruder was a night-owl who often remained online into the early morning. What's more, the information stashed in the WELL accounts included software that controls the operations of cellular phones made by various manufacturers—exactly the sort of information that interested Mitnick.

SHIMOMURA GETS HIS MAN

Just show him the money

Mitnick was apparently not interested in profiting from his computer hacking. Although he stole more than twenty-one thousand credit card numbers, authorities believe that he never used *any* of them.

Working with government investigators, Shimomura's team compared telephone company records with records of the intruder's activity on the Internet. Soon, they determined that the hacker was using a telephone switching office in Raleigh, North Carolina, to re-route phone calls—making it difficult to trace calls from his cellular phone modem. On Sunday, February 12, Shimomura flew to Raleigh, where he met a Sprint cellular technician. The pair drove through the streets of suburban Raleigh with high-tech scanning and homing equipment designed to locate the origin of the cellular modem activity. By early Monday morning, Shimomura and the technician concluded that the calls originated from an apartment complex near the Raleigh airport.

Earlier that month, a man who identified himself as Glenn Thomas Case had rented a one-bedroom apartment at the Players Club complex. When federal agents knocked on the door of apartment 202 at 2 A.M. on February 15, they found Kevin Mitnick. Although it took him five minutes to open the door to his apartment, Mitnick surrendered without a struggle. As he waited to be charged in a North Carolina jail, he was allowed a few phone calls—to his attorney, his mother, and his grandmother. All of his calls were monitored. Charged with computer fraud and illegal use of telephone-access devices, Mitnick faced up to thirty-five years in prison.

Burning the midnight oil

Mitnick was a night-owl who liked to sleep late. He typically logged on in the mid-afternoon and remained active (except for a dinner break) through the night and into the following morning. Because of his unusual schedule, the surveillance team that monitored his activities often had to work twenty-hour days.

Sources for Further Reading

Hafner, Katie. "Kevin Mitnick, Unplugged." *Esquire* (August 1995), p. 80 l .

Hafner, Katie. "A Superhacker Meets His Match." *Newsweek* (February 27, 1995), p. 61+.

Hafner, Katie and John Markoff. *Cyberpunk: Outlaws and Hackers on the Computer Frontier.* New York: Simon & Schuster, 1991.

"Interview with the Cybersleuth." *Newsweek* (March 6, 1995), p. 76.

Kennedy, Dana. "Takedown: The Pursuit and Capture of Kevin Mitnick." *Entertainment Weekly* (February 2, 1996), p. 50+.

Littman, Jonathon. "Hacked, Cracked and Phreaked." *PC Week* (January 27, 1997), p. 1+.

Markoff, John. "How a Computer Sleuth Traced a Digital Trail." *The New York Times* (February 16, 1995), p. D17.

Markoff, John. "A Most-wanted Cyberthief is Caught In His Own Web." *The New York Times* (February 16, 1995), pp. A1, D17.

A hacker's revenge

Mitnick sometimes used his hacking skills to pay back people who offended him. For example, the judge who sentenced him to serve time in a juvenile hall detention center for stealing technical information from Pacific Bell Telephone Company later discovered that his credit information had been altered. A probation officer who was involved in the case reported that his telephone was disconnected with no explanation. And police computers mysteriously lost all record of Mitnick's crimes.

Meyer, Michael. "Is This Hacker Evil or Merely Misunderstood? Two Writers Clash Over the Crimes of Kevin Mitnick." *Newsweek* (December 4, 1995), p. 60.

"Mitnick Confesses: 'No One is Secure.'" *Datamation* (January 15, 1996), p. 6+.

O'Brien, Miles. "Book Presents Two Sides of Super-Hacker Mitnick." [Online] Available http://www.cnn.com/tech/9602/hacker/index.html, January 7, 1997.

Quittner, Joshua. "Kevin Mitnick's Digital Obsession." *Time* (February 27, 1995), p. 45.

Shapiro, Andrew L. "Cyberscoop!" *The Nation* (March 20, 1995), p. 369+.

Shimomura, Tsutomu. *Takedown: The Pursuit and Capture of Kevin Mitnick, America's Most Wanted Computer Outlaw, By the Man Who Did It.* New York: Hyperion, 1996.

Sussman, Vic. "Gotcha! A Hard-core Hacker is Nabbed." *U.S. News & World Report* (February 27, 1995), p. 66+.

Stanley Rifkin

Born: 1946

Stanley Mark Rifkin, a mild-mannered computer wizard, used his skills to pull off the largest bank robbery in the history of the United States. Adding insult to injury, the bank was unaware that it had been victimized until federal officials informed them of Rifkin's scam.

AN ARTFUL SCHMOOZER

In 1978, Rifkin operated a computer consulting firm out of his apartment in the San Fernando Valley in southern California. The balding thirty-two-year-old had numerous clients, including a company that serviced the computers of the Security Pacific National Bank, headquartered in Los Angeles, California. Located in a room on the bank's D-level was Operations Unit One—a wire transfer room. A nationwide electronic wire network allows banks—including Security Pacific—to transfer money from one bank to another. Operated by the Federal Reserve Board, a government agency, the network allows banks to transfer funds throughout the United States and abroad. Like other banks, Security Pacific guarded against wire theft by using a numerical code to authorize transactions. The code changed on a daily basis.

Rifkin used his position as a consultant at the bank—and his knowledge of computers and bank practices—to rob the institution. In October 1978, he visited Security Pacific, where bank employees easily recognized him as a computer worker. He took an elevator to the D-level, where the bank's wire transfer room was located. A pleasant and friendly young man, he managed to talk his way into the room where the bank's secret code-of-the-day was posted on the wall. Rifkin memorized the code and left without arousing suspicion.

Soon, bank employees in the transfer room received a phone call from a man who identified himself as Mike Hansen, an employee of the bank's international division. The man ordered a routine transfer of funds into an account at the Irving Trust Company in New York—and he provided the secret code numbers to authorize the transaction. Nothing about the transfer appeared to be out of the ordinary, and Security Pacific transferred the money to the New York bank. What bank officials did not know was that the man who called himself Mike Hansen was in fact Stanley Rifkin, and he had used the bank's security code to rob the bank of $10.2 million.

DIAMONDS: AN UNTRACEABLE COMMODITY

Officials at Security Pacific were not aware of the theft until Federal Bureau of Investigation (FBI) agents informed them of the robbery. The heist went through without a problem—until the second part of Rifkin's plan came into play. Rifkin had actually begun preparations for the robbery in the summer of 1978, when he asked attorney Gary Goodgame for advice in finding an untraceable commodity. Goodgame suggested that Rifkin should speak to Lon Stein, a well-respected diamond dealer in Los Angeles.

In early October, Rifkin laid the groundwork to convert stolen funds into diamonds. Claiming to be a representative of a reputable firm—Coast Diamond Distributors—he contacted Stein. He claimed to be interested in placing a multi-million dollar order for diamonds. Suspecting nothing, Stein ordered diamonds through a Soviet government trading firm called Russalmaz.

On October 14, the Russalmaz office in Geneva, Switzerland, received a phone call from a man who claimed to be an

employee of the Security Pacific National Bank. The man, who called himself Mr. Nelson, informed the Russalmaz firm that Stein was acting as a representative of Coast Diamond Distributors. Further, he confirmed that Security Pacific had the funds to finance the multi-million dollar transaction. The man who called himself Mr. Nelson called again, to say that Stein would stop by Russalmaz's Geneva office on October 26 in order to look over the diamonds.

ON THE ROCKS

On October 26, Stein arrived at the Geneva office of Russalmaz. He spent that day inspecting diamonds and returned the following day with another man. (The identity of the second man is unknown. According to physical descriptions of the man, he did not resemble Rifkin.) Stein agreed to pay the Soviet firm $8.145 million in exchange for 43,200 carats of diamonds. (Diamonds are weighed by a basic unit called a carat, which is two hundred milligrams. A well-cut round diamond of one carat measures almost exactly one-quarter inch in diameter.)

Somehow Rifkin managed to smuggle the diamonds into the United States. Five days after he robbed Security Pacific, he began to sell the Soviet diamonds. First, he sold twelve diamonds to a jeweler in Beverly Hills—an exclusive suburb of Los Angeles, California—for $12,000. Next, he traveled to Rochester, New York, where he attempted to sell more of the diamonds. There Rifkin's plot hit a snag.

On November 1, he visited Paul O'Brien, a former business associate. He informed O'Brien that he had received diamonds as payment for a West German real estate deal—and that he wanted to exchange the diamonds for cash. Before he had a chance to act on Rifkin's request, O'Brien saw a news item on television describing a multimillion-dollar bank heist in Los Angeles. The story named Rifkin as the thief. O'Brien wasted no time in contacting the FBI.

CONVICTED OF WIRE FRAUD

Rifkin flew to San Diego, California, to spend a weekend with Daniel Wolfson, an old friend. He informed Wolfson that he planned to surrender. But he never had the opportunity to give himself up. O'Brien had given the FBI permission to record calls from Rifkin. On November 5, Rifkin called O'Brien. The conversation contained information that allowed FBI agents to track Rifkin to Wolfson's Carslbad, California, address.

Around midnight on Sunday, November 5, FBI agents Robin Brown and Norman Wight appeared at Wolfson's apartment. At first, Wolfson barred their entry with outstretched arms. When the agents informed him that they would force their way inside if necessary, he allowed them to enter. Rifkin surrendered without a struggle. He also turned over evidence to the federal agents: a suitcase containing the $12,000 from the Beverly Hills diamond sale and several dozen packets of diamonds that had been hidden in a plastic shirt cover.

Rifkin was taken to the Metropolitan Correctional Center in San Diego. Soon after he was released on bail, he got into more trouble with the FBI. He had begun to target the Union Bank of Los Angeles—using the same scheme that had worked at the Security Pacific National Bank. What he did not know was that someone involved in the scheme was a government informant who had set him up. Rifkin was arrested again on February 13, 1979. Federal agents also arrested Patricia Ferguson, who was helping Rifkin set-up the bank. Tried on two counts of wire fraud, Rifkin faced the possibility of ten years imprisonment. He pleaded guilty, and on March 26, 1979, was sentenced to eight years in federal prison. In June 1979, Ferguson was convicted of three counts of conspiracy.

A picture worth a thousand words

Rifkin was picked up by FBI agents at the home of Daniel Wolfson. Wolfson, a photographer, shot pictures of his old school pal as federal agents escorted him into custody. He sold the photographs the following day for $250. One of the photographs was purchased by UPI (United Press International). The picture included the caption: "Stanley Mark Rifkin, 32, smiles in this picture, taken minutes after his arrest, by Dan Wolfson, who rented the apartment where Rifkin was arrested. Rifkin, a computer wizard, is charged with defrauding a Los Angeles bank of $10.2 million. Wolfson was also arrested . . . during the telephone interview with UPI." Wolfson was later charged with harboring a criminal.

Sources for Further Reading

Nash, Jay Robert. *The Encyclopedia of World Crime.* Wilmette, IL: Crime Books, 1990, pp. 2582–2583.

"The Ultimate Heist." *Time* (November 20, 1978), p. 48.

Jerry Schneider

Active: Early 1970s

Working a loophole in the system to his advantage, Jerry Neal Schneider employed the telephone to steal thousands of dollars worth of products from the Pacific Bell Telephone & Telegraph Company. He ordered at will, never paying for the products—until two of his employees blew the whistle on his illegal operation.

A PHONE FANATIC

By the time he was four years old, Schneider was shy and overweight. Growing up he had no real friends. Other children called him "fatso." He loved telephones and by the time he was ten, he had built a telecommunications system in his family's home. A few years later, he received a telephone repair worker's belt and hat—so that he could pretend to be a repair man. Talented in science, Schneider won prizes at science fairs. First a ham radio operator, Schneider eventually became a "phone phreak"—someone who illegally uses telephone company services.

As a student at Hamilton High in Los Angeles, California, Schneider was president of the radio club. He once asked officials at Pacific Telephone & Telegraph (PT&T) Company to give him phone company equipment for his electronics class. The phone company refused. He later applied for a job with PT&T—and again, he was refused.

Fifteen minutes of fame-- and then some

Catapulted to fame by his brazen use of electronics to steal hundreds of thousands of dollars worth of computer equipment from the Pacific Telephone & Telegraph Company, Schneider instantly became a media hit. On October 10, 1976—more than four years after he was released from prison—Schneider appeared on a *60 Minutes* television segment called "Dial E for Embezzlement." (Embezzlement involves swindling money by violating a trust.)

Dan Rather, the host of *60 Minutes,* introduced the segment with these words: "The way a banker makes money is to move money around as fast as he can. Bankers are hell-bent to speed up their systems with instant communications and electronic wizardry. Trouble is, the bank thieves are as up-to-date as the bankers, and sometimes a step ahead. . . . Faster banking can lead to faster stealing, as some sadder and wiser banks are beginning to learn."

Next, Rather introduced Schneider, a convicted computer thief. "Sometimes," Rather said, "it takes a thief to catch a thief." By the end of the segment, Schneider had used his phone phreaking skills to prove Rather's point. Armed with nothing more than a phone number and a credit card number, Schneider had gotten the bank to raise Rather's credit limit from $500 to $10,000!

IN BUSINESS FOR HIMSELF

In spite of the obstacles he encountered, Schneider was determined to get into the telephone business. While in high school, he regularly passed by the PT&T warehouse. He examined the contents of the warehouse dumpster and found operating manuals and specific instructions for ordering computer equipment by phone. After graduating, he studied engineering and used the PT&T materials to start up a small business.

Pretending to be a company supplier, Schneider ordered computer equipment over the telephone—using the ordering guidelines from the instructions he had taken from the dumpster. First, he consulted a PT&T catalog for the seven-digit code number for a product he wanted to order. Next, he punched in his order using a PT&T telephone that allowed him to order directly through the company's computerized inventory system. Schneider and his employees then picked up the merchandise that had been ordered. To almost everyone concerned, the business appeared to be legitimate. Assisted by ten employees,

Phone phreaking

Schneider once told a reporter at the *Los Angeles Times,* "Phone phreaking didn't prove to be any great challenge to me. . . . I was more into setting up large-scale computer systems."

A hacker's dictionary

Diddling: To deliberately change the information that is stored on a network by erasing or changing data. When a hacker named Susan Thunder and her friends replaced financial information with swear words, they were diddling.

Eavesdropping: To poke around a system's software and data and to read private information such as e-mail, financial information, and other non-public material.

Scavenging: To get hold of information as it was being discarded or transferred from one system to another. Schneider used information he had scavenged from the Pacific Bell Telephone & Telegraph company to supply his illegal business. *Dumpster diving* is a common form of scavenging.

Spoofing: To fool a computer into thinking you are an authorized user to gain improper access to a system.

Superzap: To use unauthorized means to bypass passwords and other security measures to gain access to private computer files.

Salami: To steal small amounts of assets from many large accounts.

Schneider conducted his business out of a six-thousand- square-foot warehouse.

DISGRUNTLED EMPLOYEES

Not everyone was convinced that Schneider's business was legal. Special agents at the phone company had received word from one of Schneider's customers that he was selling phone company merchandise. For nearly three months they tracked his activities, but were unable to gather solid evidence against him.

Just before Christmas 1971, one of Schneider's employees, John Nicholas, contacted PT&T officials. Nicholas claimed that Schneider had hired him in September as a warehouse manager. Soon after he started his new job, he began to suspect foul play. Nicholas said that Schneider claimed to have received a shipment of phone company equipment from a salvage center—but many of the products looked brand-new. Schneider loaded shipments into a truck that was the same make and style as phone company vehicles—but it was not an official PT&T vehicle. He told officials that he was given an official PT&T purchase order form—but he never signed any receipts for the shipments he picked up.

Eventually, Nicholas and another employee, Earl Eugene Watson, confronted Schneider. The two men gave Schneider a choice: either abandon all illegal practices or suffer the consequences. Schneider reportedly told the two employees that it would be impossible to turn a profit by running a legitimate business. He promised to close down his operation. When he didn't, Nicholas and Watson informed the authorities about their former boss's illegal activities.

A COMPUTER-AGE SHERLOCK HOLMES

Based on these reports, Los Angeles district attorney investigators Frank Kovacevich, Ron Maus, and others arrived at Schneider's office with a search warrant. They found a stash of inventory. Schneider immediately became front-page news. The February 9, 1972, edition of the *Los Angeles Times* carried a story whose headline—"Massive Phone Thefts Uncovered"—stretched across the entire front page. One article called Schneider a computer-age Sherlock Holmes; another was titled "How to Steal a Million from a Computer."

Officials at PT&T filed a lawsuit against Schneider's operation—based only on the inventory that had been found at Schneider's office. (Early estimates placed the phone company's losses at hundreds of thousands of dollars.) Schneider pleaded guilty to receiving stolen property. He was sentenced to less than two months at a low-security prison farm in southern California and was ordered to pay the PT&T company $8,500.

Following his release from prison, Schneider claimed to have gone into computer security consulting (although no one ever actually paid him for his services). Next, he became involved in offshore banking—an enterprise that sometimes treads a fine line between legitimate and illegal business.

Phone phreaks

A phone phreak is a hacker who specializes in breaking into telephone systems. Among other things, phone phreaks figure out how to use the telephone company's long distance service without paying for it. In the early days of phone phreaking, hackers used a "blue box"—a device that imitated a high-pitched tone in the switching system—to trick the telephone service into providing toll-free long-distance calls. (The founders of the Apple Computer Company—Stephen Jobs and Steve Wozniak—were among the many college students who sold home-made blue boxes for spending money.) By the middle of the 1970s, phone phreaking was so widely practiced that the American Telephone & Telegraph company (AT&T) reported losing about $30 million each year to phone fraud.

Sources for Further Reading

Nash, Jay Robert. *The Encyclopedia of World Crime.* Wilmette, IL: Crime Books, 1990, p. 2696.

Parker, Donn B. *Crime by Computer.* New York: Charles Scribner's Sons, 1976, pp. 59–70.

Reen, Brian. *True Hackers are not Dangerous.* [Online] Available http://www.cedarville.edu/student/s1143400/hack.htm, December 2, 1997.

Spies

Spying entails watching in secret—usually for hostile purposes. The spy's motives may involve political and ideological concerns—or simple financial gain. And his or her methods often involve exploiting a position of trust. Elizabeth Van Lew used her position in the community to spy on the Confederate war effort. Christopher Boyce took advantage of his job at an aerospace firm to pass classified information to Soviet agents. Julius and Ethel Rosenberg used a family connection to gain access to the nation's top-secret atomic bomb project. Some spied for profit and others believed they were acting for the greater good. They were regarded as heroes, or traitors—or both. In this section you'll encounter a CIA mole, an FBI double-agent, a Soviet agent who disappeared without a trace from her New York apartment, and others. You'll find out what they did, why they did it, and the price they paid for engaging in espionage.

Aldrich Ames

Born: May 26, 1941

During his thirty-two year career at the CIA, Aldrich Hazen Ames was known as a mediocre agent who tended to drink too much. What Ames's superiors did not know was worse than that: he was, from 1985 to 1994, a mole (spy) who passed top-level national secrets to the Soviet Union.

First contact

Ames's role as a Soviet mole began in April 1985. In order to create a legitimate reason to visit the Soviet embassy in Washington, D.C., he arranged to meet with Sergei Chuvakin, an embassy diplomat who was an expert on nuclear weapons. Ames told the Soviet diplomat that he wanted to meet in order to discuss foreign policy issues. He told his superiors at the CIA that he had arranged the meeting in order to attempt to recruit Chuvakin (to spy for the U.S.). But in truth, he arranged the meeting to provide a cover for the real reason he visited the Soviet embassy: to contact the Soviet secret police (known as the KGB) and offer his services.

Before Ames met with Chuvakin at the Soviet embassy, he stopped briefly at the desk of the embassy receptionist. Without speaking, he passed her an envelope. Addressed to a senior KGB officer, the envelope contained three items: the names of three Soviets who had offered to work for the CIA; a page from the CIA directory, with Ames's name highlighted; and a demand for

Double jeopardy

From late 1985 to early 1986, the Central Intelligence Agency (CIA) lost most of its agents in the Soviet Union. Three dozen operatives were sent to prison—or executed—as a result of information that Ames provided to the Soviet espionage service (also known as the KGB). The execution of two operatives—Valeri Martynov and Sergei Motorin—alerted the CIA to the possibility that a mole (spy) was leaking government secrets to the Soviets.

In the summer of 1980, U.S. officials had persuaded Sergei Motorin, a young major in the KGB, to spy for them. FBI officials knew that Motorin had been involved in a car accident—and that a prostitute had been a passenger in his car. They also knew that the Soviet agent had attempted to trade his government allotment (allowance) of vodka and cigars for stereo equipment in a store in downtown Washington. Motorin's superiors would frown on such behavior. Armed with this information, FBI officials convinced the Soviet to spy for them. Although slow to agree, Motorin eventually provided agents with the name of every KGB operative in the Soviet embassy in Washington, D.C. Motorin returned to Moscow at the end of 1984, six months before Ames provided information to the Soviets that identified him as a double-agent. He was executed.

Valeri Martynov arrived in Washington, in November 1980, to assume the post of third secretary of the Soviet embassy there. Martynov's title was a cover for his real position as a lieutenant colonel in the KGB. The Soviet agent began to supply United States intelligence officials with secret information after he was recruited in the spring of 1982. Ames provided the KGB with information about Martynov's activities. Ordered to return to Moscow in November 1985, Martynov remained in jail until he was executed by a firing squad on May 28, 1987, at the age of forty-one.

$50,000. The names offered proof that he had access to valuable information. The directory page provided evidence that he was in a position to gather more information. And the demand for payment made clear his intentions.

Two days after his first meeting with Chuvakin on April 16, 1985, Ames deposited $9,000 in cash into one of his two accounts at the Dominion Bank of Virginia. Two months later, he marched by security guards at the CIA headquarters with plastic bags filled with several pounds of classified documents. He delivered the bags to the KGB. The documents contained a wealth of valuable information, including the names of ten Soviets who were acting as double agents (agents working for a government that they were actually spying on), providing Western intelligence agencies with Soviet secrets.

On August 10, 1985, Ames married a Colombian woman named Maria del Rosario Casas. (He had recently divorced his first wife, Nan, who was also a CIA employee.) By the time he and his new wife traveled to Rome, Italy, where Ames would spend a three-year term in a program to recruit more spies from the Soviet embassy, his bank deposits amounted to $123,500—a rather sudden increase in income for a $69,000-a-year government agent.

AN INFORMATION LEAK

The Soviets did not ignore the information that Ames passed to them. They jailed and executed the men who were identified as double agents. Eventually the CIA received news that two Soviet agents—Valeri Martynov and Sergei Motorin—had been returned to Moscow and executed. Officials began to suspect a leak within the CIA. At first they investigated the possibility that the Soviets were intercepting CIA communications. In order to test this theory, officials sent a number of phony messages that were designed to stir up a reaction in the KGB organization. But the KGB did nothing.

Slowly, CIA officials admitted that someone within their own organization was responsible for the leak. In January 1986, the agency attempted to reduce the possibility of further leaks by limiting access to top-secret information to a small group of officers. The new procedure might have worked—had Ames not been one of the officers who received top-level clearance.

AT THE TOP OF THE SPY LIST

U.S. investigators were not sure whether they were looking for one spy or more. The Federal Bureau of Investigation (FBI) worked with the CIA to investigate the problem. FBI agents compiled two "bigot lists" of possible suspects. One list contained "single suspects" who might have worked alone, while

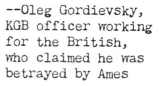

Murderous intent

"[Ames] has the blood of a dozen officers on his hands. He would have had my blood, too, had I not managed to escape."

--Oleg Gordievsky, KGB officer working for the British, who claimed he was betrayed by Ames

I AM READY TO MEET
AT B ON 1 OCT.
    I CANNOT READ
NORTH 13-19 SEPT.
    IF YOU WILL
MEET AT B ON 1 OCT.
PLS SIGNAL NORTH 4
OF 20 SEPT TO CONFI.
NO MESSAGE AT PIPE.
    IF YOU CANNOT MEE.
1 OCT, SIGNAL NORTH AFTER
27 SEPT WITH MESSAGE AT
PIPE.

30917045 D ZU Q4

FBI
LABORATORY

This torn note, found in Ames's garbage, was the first evidence that he was meeting with the Russians.

the other list provided the names of agents who might have worked together to spy for the Soviets. Ames was on both lists.

To be named on a list, an agent must have had access to information on a case that failed. Investigators also took into account other factors—such as a drinking or drug problem, unexplained time away from work or home, or a lifestyle that exceeded the suspect's income. Ames had a well-documented drinking problem. He drove an expensive red Jaguar and had paid cash for a luxurious $540,000 home. He had expensive tastes—which ranged from original art work to Swiss-made watches. And his bank accounts showed numerous large cash deposits. Ames began to move to the top of investigators' lists of suspects.

A MOLE HUNT

The FBI began to focus on Ames. On May 12, 1993, they opened a criminal investigation of the Soviet mole suspect. In an operation whose code-name was "Nightmover," agents monitored Ames's telephone conversations at home and in his car. They raided his garbage on a regular basis. Posing as lawn workers and tree trimmers, they installed a small video camera in a neighbor's tree to monitor Ames's comings and goings. And finally they entered his home.

On October 9, 1993—while Ames and his wife and child spent a long weekend in Florida—agents entered his house with a search warrant that had been authorized by Attorney General Janet Reno. One agent examined Ames's bank books to look for suspicious deposits. A computer whiz named Tom Murray broke into Ames's personal computer. He found messages about message relays, meetings, and document transfers. And he found file after file of top-secret CIA information that should never have found its way to Ames's home computer. What they found left no doubt: Ames was the Soviet mole.

Aldrich Ames and his wife, Rosario, are escorted from the courthouse by federal marshals on March 10, 1994.

A CONVICTED TRAITOR

Agents were reluctant to arrest Ames. Although they had plenty of evidence against him, they had not caught him in the act of selling national secrets to the Soviets. But they couldn't afford to wait until Ames tipped his hand. Involving more than one hundred special agents, the spy-catching operation could

What is the truth?

Officials in the CIA and FBI are not sure whether to believe Ames about when he was recruited by the Soviets—and why he became a double-agent. Ames claimed that he became a Soviet spy in 1985—and that he was motivated primarily by greed. But when Ames underwent a polygraph (lie-detector exam), he failed questions about his recruitment and his motivations.

not be hidden from Ames indefinitely. And even if Ames didn't become suspicious, his neighbors were bound to notice odd activities around the government man's house.

And there was the question of whether Ames planned to defect (to desert one's country). The FBI noticed that Russian intelligence officers had been passing through Ames's neighborhood with increasing frequency. What's more, Ames had scheduled a business trip to Moscow—which would provide him with the opportunity to defect to the Soviet Union.

Ames was arrested on a quiet suburban street on February 21, 1994, as he drove from his home to CIA headquarters. Ames pleaded guilty, was convicted of espionage, and was sentenced to life imprisonment. His wife, Rosario, who knew of Ames's activities, was sentenced to five years and three months. Unapologetic about the deaths he caused, Ames claimed that money was his main motivation, coupled with a strong disregard for the foreign policy of President Ronald Reagan's administration and a conviction that spying for the CIA had no meaning. He was quoted as saying, "This is the great myth of espionage: that it makes a difference. Of course, it doesn't."

DEADLY INFORMATION

Over the nine-year period during which Ames acted as a government mole, he collected $2.5 million for information he sold to the Russians. The information he sold exposed more than one hundred intelligence operations and led to the execution of at least ten top spies. "They died," former CIA Director James Woolsey claimed, "because this warped, murdering traitor wanted a bigger house and a Jaguar."

Sources for Further Reading

"The Aldrich Ames Holiday Shopping Guide." *Time* (December 5, 1994), p. 25.

Corn, David. "A Talk with Aldrich Ames." *The Nation* (September 11, 1995), p. 238+.

Duffy, Brian. "The Cold War's Last Spy." *U.S. News & World Report* (March 6, 1995), p. 48+.

Earley, Pete. *Confessions of a Spy: The Real Story of Aldrich Ames.* New York: G. P. Putnam's Sons, 1997.

Pound, Edward T. "The Spy Who Picked the CIA's Pockets." *U.S. News & World Report* (May 9, 1994), p. 49.

Thomas, Evan. "Spooking the Director." *Newsweek* (November 6, 1995), p. 42+.

"Victims of Aldrich Ames." *Time* (May 22, 1995), p. 56.

Waller, Douglas. "For Your Disinformation." *Time* (November 13, 1995), p. 82.

Hundreds of suspects

When the FBI began to investigate the intelligence leaks that had led to the execution of two operatives, Ames was only one of hundreds of suspects. Edward Lee Howard, an agent who had defected to Moscow in September 1985, was an early prime suspect.

Christopher Boyce and Andrew Daulton Lee

Christopher Boyce: 1953–
Andrew Daulton Lee: 1952–

Boyhood friends Christopher Boyce and Andrew Daulton Lee shared several things— including a privileged upbringing, involvement with drugs, and discontent with the U.S. government. Together, they spied for Soviet intelligence, for which U.S. officials estimated they received $17,500. Discovered by chance, each turned against the other— and both earned extended prison terms.

PALS IN PALOS VERDES

Boyce and Lee both grew up in Palos Verdes—one of the wealthiest suburbs in southern California. Lee's adoptive father was a successful physician; Boyce was the son of an Federal Bureau of Investigation (FBI) agent who later took a higher paying job as the security director of McDonnell Douglas Corporation, an airplane manufacturer. The two boys met at a local Catholic church while serving as altar boys and soon became good friends. They spent much of their free time with one another, and both shared an intense interest in falconry—the art of training falcons, or hawks.

Lee, a gifted woodworker, had little interest in school. He became increasingly involved with drugs as a teenager, and eventually went into business selling them with a young man named Cameron Adams. Buying and selling cocaine and marijuana, the pair earned $2,000 a week. By 1977, Lee had been arrested five times for possessing and selling drugs—and three times for driving under the influence of alcohol or drugs. He also had one arrest for suspicion of robbery and resisting arrest.

One of Lee's arrests—for selling cocaine to undercover agents working for the Los Angeles County sheriff's department—earned him a one-year jail sentence. From jail, he wrote to a judge begging to be set free so that he could continue his education. He wrote, "My incarceration [imprisonment] has helped me to evaluate my life and made it possible for me to formulate plans for the future." Released after seven months in prison, Lee enrolled in a nearby junior college—and then dropped out. He returned to selling drugs and, since he violated the terms of his probation, a warrant was issued for his arrest.

Boyce had no police record. He was an intelligent young man whose IQ (intelligence quotient) of 142 was well above average. When he put his mind to it, he earned straight-As in school. The oldest of nine children, he was a devout Catholic and was well-liked by neighbors who saw him as an idealistic young man. Although he was a bright student, Boyce was not eager to attend college. After enrolling and dropping out three times over the course of three years, he took a job in nearby Redondo Beach, California.

INSIDE THE BLACK VAULT

On July 29, 1974, Boyce began work at TRW Systems, Inc., an aerospace firm that worked on many classified military programs. TRW was one of two companies that manufactured most of the "spy" satellites for the Central Intelligence Agency (CIA). Boyce earned $140 per week as a communications clerk at TRW. Within months, he was responsible for running the company's "black vault"—a high-security operation that involved top-secret information. Awarded top-secret clearance, he supervised secret communications between TRW and the CIA headquarters in Langley, Virginia. Boyce operated two types of coding systems that transmitted information involving TRW satellites. He also handled coded material concerning top-secret Air Force, Army, and Navy communications.

> ### Take a look at this!
>
> *The Falcon and the Snowman* (1985), based on the book by the same name, tells of boyhood friends Christopher Boyce and Andrew Daulton Lee. The movie features Sean Penn as Lee and Timothy Hutton as Boyce.

U.S. Espionage Act

Boyce and Lee were both tried under the United States Espionage Act--the same law that sent convicted spies, **Ethel and Julius Rosenberg** (see entry) to their deaths.

Andrew Daulton Lee.

Few people received the security clearance required to enter the black vault. And fewer still received clearance to handle coded material contained in the vault. CIA officials routinely conducted extensive background checks of employees before granting them security clearance. Why Boyce—a twenty-one-year-old high school graduate—received clearance has puzzled authorities. Many have suggested that it was no coincidence that Boyce's father was a friend of Regis Carr—a former FBI agent who was in charge of "special projects" security at TRW.

CODE NAME "LUIS"

At some point in 1975, Boyce and Lee devised a plan to provide Soviet agents with top-secret information. How the plan started—and whose idea it was—has become the subject of debate. During 1975, Lee traveled to the Soviet embassy in Mexico City, Mexico, a center of Soviet espionage activities. He informed the Russians that he was working with someone who had access to top-secret information on U.S. spy satellites. Further, he said that he wanted to sell them classified information, and offered two documents as proof that he could deliver valuable information.

After five hours of questioning, the Soviets informed Lee that they were interested in his proposition. Lee's contact was Boris A. Grishin, the embassy's science attaché. Grishin was, in fact, an agent in the KGB—the Soviet espionage service. Grishin informed Lee that they were to refer to each other by code names: the Soviet agent would go by the name "John," while Lee would take the code-name "Luis."

Over the course of eighteen months, Lee provided Soviet agents with information Boyce smuggled out of TRW. He made several trips to Mexico, and traveled to Vienna, Austria, where Soviet agents had arranged to meet him to avoid surveillance. Using a camera Lee had purchased with money from the Soviets, Boyce photographed sensitive documents in the security vault. Some documents he smuggled off company grounds by placing them inside potted plants.

TROUBLE IN MEXICO

In December 1976, Boyce left TRW. But Lee had one final delivery to make to the Soviet embassy. On January 6, 1977, he followed the usual procedure to arrange a meeting with "John." First he taped a large "X" on a lamp post, as he had many times before. Later that evening, he waited for Grishin at the Viva Pizza Restaurant. After his contact failed to appear, he followed a backup plan: he returned to the pre-arranged meeting spot the following morning. Again, Grishin did not appear.

Next, Lee went to the Soviet embassy—although he had been specifically warned not to. The Soviet embassy was normally monitored by Mexican police. When he

Christopher Boyce.

threw an envelope over the embassy's fence, police suspected that he might have thrown a bomb onto the embassy grounds. Lee was taken to police headquarters and forced to empty his pockets. What the Mexican police found aroused their interest: inside an envelope Lee was carrying were twenty strips of film that contained photographs of documents—all of which were marked "TOP SECRET." The film reportedly contained a feasibility study (a study to determine whether something can be accomplished) of a spy communications satellite network that operated through miniature receiver/transmitters in the Soviet Union and China.

At first Lee protested that the films were part of an ad campaign for the General Electric Company. But Mexican police notified officials at the U.S. Embassy in Mexico City, who in turn notified the CIA. Boyce and Lee's spy operation immediately began to unravel. Lee informed on Boyce, who was picked up ten days later by FBI agents in Los Angeles. Boyce, in turn, confessed that he had copied the documents that Lee provided to the Soviets.

Letter from prison

On the night before his trial began, Boyce wrote a letter to his father from prison. It explained, in part, why he had gotten involved in espionage.

Dear Dad:

I thought of you all long and hard today and have decided I owe you an explanation of my feelings. In reality I owe you so much more than that, but at this point it is all I can give.

I wish I could bring myself to convey my love to my family from this place but I cannot and so I leave it up to you. I realized many dozens of months ago that there could be no coming back from the decisions made and I do not propose to pick up the pieces now. I regret none of my actions except for the deceptions that I played upon you [and] any subsequent loss of face. For that I am truly sorry, more now than ever. If we never understood each other, the fault is mine. . . .

To my perceptions, the foundations of this country are a sham. It was designed by the few for the few and so it will remain. Western culture is in decline now and the trend cannot be reversed. We are grasping alone in a headless insanity that will continue to consume until nothing is left.

CONVICTED SPIES

Boyce and Lee were accused of spying for the Soviets. Although they were tried separately, both were prosecuted under the United States Espionage Act in April 1977. Boyce claimed that he had been bullied by Lee into spying for the Soviets—and that he was afraid of being blackmailed by his former partner. He even volunteered to take a lie detector test to prove that he was telling the truth. Boyce was convicted—on eight counts of espionage, conspiracy to commit espionage, and theft of official documents—and sentenced to forty years in prison.

Less than three years later—in January 1980—he escaped from a high-security federal prison in Lompoc, California, by cutting through barbed wire fences. Nineteen months later—after a series of robberies—he was captured by FBI agents in a fishing port sixty miles north of Seattle, Washington. When Boyce returned to prison, ninety years had been added to his sentence for additional charges of conspiracy, firearms violations, and robbery.

Time and time again I watched the destruction of those things and places I love and I was disgusted. I believe we are on the edge of a poisoned horrible darkness. Industrialism and technology are dragging humanity toward universal collapse and will take most life forms with it. . . .

I would give anything to be out of this place and be able to feel sunshine and to just even run again. I think there is small chance of that now so I have detached myself from what goes on here.

Being alone all the time leaves one much time to turn thoughts inward. As I think back upon my beliefs that put me here in the first place, they are strengthened more than ever. I could never make of my life that which you would have wanted.

That is no reflection on you. I chose freely my response to this absurd world, and if given the opportunity again, I would be even more vigorous. Please give all my love to mom and Kathy and everyone and tell them for me to see them would just make a bad situation worse.

Respectfully,

Chris

Lee's defense was widely viewed as ridiculous. He claimed that he thought that he was part of an undercover CIA operation to provide Soviet agents with inaccurate information. He was convicted of espionage and sentenced to life in prison.

Sources for Further Reading

Lindsey, Robert. *The Falcon and the Snowman.* New York: Simon & Schuster, 1979, pp. 356–357.

Lindsey, Robert. "To be young, rich—and a spy." *The New York Times Magazine* (May 22, 1977), p. 18.

Nash, Jay Robert. *Spies: A Narrative Encyclopedia of Dirty Deeds and Double Dealing from Biblical Times to Today.* New York: M. Evans, 1997, pp. 113–115.

"Stealing the Company Store." *Time* (May 9, 1977), p. 19.

Steele, Richard. "The 'Pyramider' Spy Case." *Newsweek* (April 18, 1977), p. 29.

Juliet Stuart Poyntz

Born: November 25, 1886
Died: 1937?

A former member of the Communist Party, Juliet Stuart Poyntz was trained in Soviet espionage. After brief service as a spy for the Soviets, she became disillusioned and announced her plan to retire—and was never heard from again.

A WELL-EDUCATED WOMAN

Poyntz was born on November 25, 1886, in Omaha, Nebraska, to an Irish Catholic family. Her parents were Alice E. Poyntz and John J. Poyntz, a lawyer. An intellectually gifted young woman, Poyntz graduated from Barnard College with high honors in 1907. In 1910, at a time when few women pursued graduate degrees, she earned a master's degree from Columbia University in New York. She also attended the prestigious London School of Economics at London University in England (1910–1911) and Oxford University, in Oxford, England (1911–1912).

Poyntz's education enabled her to land research positions in a number of organizations. She was a special investigator for the U.S. Immigration Commission from 1908 to 1909, and a researcher for the American Association for Labor Legislation from 1910 to 1913. In 1914 she became the director of the Bureau of Labor Research at the Rand School, a position she held until 1915. She was the educational director of the International Ladies Garment Workers Union for four years, from 1915 to 1919. She also taught for a while at Columbia University, one of the nation's leading educational institutions.

Interested in social questions and social reform, Poyntz was a spokesperson for women's suffrage (right to vote). While still in her twenties, she lectured at various suffrage organizations in New York City. She also contributed articles to a number of magazines and professional publications. Awarded the first scholarship to be given by the General Federation of Women's Clubs of the United States of America, she was a member of numerous professional organizations, including the American Historical Association and the Oxford Anthropological Association.

COMMUNIST ACTIVITY

Poyntz became a member of the American Communist Party (ACP) in New York in 1921. An educated and persuasive speaker, she became a distinguished member of the ACP. Although she never rose to the highest level of leadership, she was one of the most influential women leaders in the ACP. She was a candidate for public office on the Communist Party ticket

Who killed Carlo Tresca?

The answer to that question is, most likely, the Mafia. Carlo Tresca was born the son of a wealthy landowning family in Sulmona, Italy, in 1879. By the middle of the 1890s, however, the family had lost its land and privileged status due to a series of bad investments and a poor economy. Tresca was deeply disappointed by these events. He eventually turned to anarchism as a political philosophy.

Tresca found employment as editor of the Socialist Party newspaper in Italy, but was forced to flee to America when his critical writings earned him too many enemies. In America he eventually became well known as an anti-communist and anti-fascist. (Fascism is a dictatorship of the extreme right.) In that role, he used much of his energy to rage against Italian dictator Benito Mussolini (1883–1945) in the Italian-language newspaper that he published, *Il Martello*. Mussolini had Tresca's name placed on a death list in 1931, but it was not until 1943 that the sentence was actually carried out.

Vito Genovese, a leader of the New York Mafia, had been forced to leave the United States for Italy in the 1930s in order to escape a murder charge. There he managed to develop a friendly relationship with Mussolini and the Fascist cause. After Mussolini complained to him about Tresca's anti-fascist activities in America, Genovese informed the Italian leader that he would take care of the problem.

On January 11, 1943, as Tresca crossed Fifteenth Street in New York with his friend Giuseppe Calabi, they paused under a streetlamp. Another man stepped from the darkness and shot Tresca once in the back and once in the head, killing him instantly. For several years the crime was listed as an unsolved political assassination. It is now commonly believed that Genovese ordered the killing to improve his relationship with Mussolini. The murder was reportedly carried out by Carmine Galante—who later became a Mafia leader and was himself killed in 1979.

and directed the New York Workers School. She also led the organization's Women's Department and served for a time as national secretary of the International Labor Defense.

Poyntz was an active member of the Communist Party throughout the 1920s and into the 1930s. She helped organize the Friends of the Soviet Union and the Trade Union Unity League. Her work with the Workers Committee Against Unemployment would be her last public contribution to the Communist Party.

A Soviet spy

At a time when the Soviet Union was attempting to increase its espionage (spy) base in the United States, Poyntz was recruited to work as a Soviet spy. As was routine for spies recruited from the United States, she first dropped out of the ACP—although she continued to maintain ties with her communist associates.

Sometime around 1934 or 1935, Poyntz reportedly traveled to Moscow in the Soviet Union to be trained in espionage. Poyntz was seen in Moscow in 1936. She was in the company of George Mink, an American who had been convicted of espionage in 1935 for his role as a Soviet agent. When she returned to New York, Poyntz was established in an apartment and provided with funds that allowed her to lead a comfortable existence as a spy for the Soviet Union.

Poyntz did not remain with Soviet intelligence for long. At first a devoted agent, she began to find herself at odds with Soviet policy. In 1936 and 1937, Soviet leader Joseph Stalin (1879–1953), carried out a series of "purges" to rid himself of opponents. In 1937, the Trial of the Seventeen allowed Stalin to do away with the leader of his potential opponents—that is, those who were still living. Around that time, Poyntz informed her friend Carlo Tresca that she planned to discontinue her espionage activities.

The lady vanishes

Fifty years old when she announced her resignation, Poyntz left her New York apartment. She moved into an inexpensive room at the Women's Association Clubhouse at 353 West 57th Street in New York. Sometime in late May or early June, she left her room. No one saw her leave, but she obviously planned to return. The light was on. She left all her belongings in the room. The memoirs she had been working on were spread out on a table. No note indicated where she was going or when she would return.

Poyntz never returned. And no evidence of what happened to her has ever been found. But many had theories about the

Here's a book you might like:

Who Was That Masked Man, Anyway, 1992, by Avi Wortis

A boy pretends that he is a master spy as he and his friend reenact their favorite radio serials. They spend much of their time trying to do away with the family lodger, nicknamed "the evil scientist," and to marry off the boy's older brother, a World War II veteran.

fate of the former spy. Many of Poyntz's friends blamed the Soviets for her disappearance. It was not an unusual situation: various people who were associated with communist parties in the United States and other parts of the world had been assassinated—or had vanished. Soviet agents were frequently blamed for these killings and disappearances.

Tresca, an American anarchist who often gave speeches, blamed Mink for his friend's disappearance. (Anarchists believe that all forms of government are oppressive and should be abolished.) Mink, who was believed to be an agent in the Soviet Union's secret police, had been seen in New York at the time of Poyntz's disappearance. It was not an outrageous suggestion. Mink had previously been openly accused of arranging the assassinations of two Italian anarchists. Tresca was not alone in accusing Mink of playing a role in Poyntz's disappearance. Benjamin Gitlow, a former prominent member of the ACP, also accused Mink. Tresca was assassinated in 1943.

Sources for Further Reading

Johnpoll, Bernard K. and Harvey Klehr, eds. *Biographical Dictionary of the American Left*. Westport, CT: Greenwood Press, 1986, pp. 317–318.

Leonard, John William, ed. *Woman's Who's Who of America*. Detroit: Gale, 1976, p. 659.

Nash, Jay Robert. *The Encyclopedia of World Crime*. Wilmette, IL: Crime Books, 1990, p. 2495.

Seth, Ronald. *Encyclopedia of Espionage*. London, England: New English Library, 1975, pp. 488–491.

Ethel and Julius Rosenberg

Ethel Rosenberg: 1915-1953
Julius Rosenberg: 1918-1953

Ethel and Julius Rosenberg were convicted of conspiracy to commit espionage for their supposed roles in passing atomic secrets to the Soviets. The fact that they were convicted on circumstantial evidence, and the resulting severity of their sentences, emphasizes the seriousness of the two greatest fears of the 1950s: communism and the atomic bomb.

A COMMUNIST COUPLE

Julius Rosenberg grew up in a poor and strictly religious Jewish family in New York. Although he had been trained to become a rabbi, he became involved in radical politics by the time he was a teenager. In 1936, he met his future wife, Ethel Greenglass, at a New Year's Eve benefit for the International Seamen's Union. Greenglass was a politically active New York native who helped organize labor groups. Born on New York's Lower East Side, she was the only daughter of Austrian-born Tessie Felt Greenglass and Barnet Greenglass, a Russian immigrant who repaired sewing machines from the basement of the family's tenement. Ethel had three brothers: an older half-brother, Samuel, and two younger brothers, Bernard and David.

Rosenberg, a student in electrical engineering at City College of New York, joined the Young Communist League in 1934. After he graduated from college in 1939, the couple married and moved into a small Brooklyn apartment. Rosenberg found a civilian (non-military) job as an engineer inspector for the U.S.

Army Signal Corps. For a while, both Rosenbergs were active participants in the Communist Party. They brought Ethel's brother David into the party and, later, David's wife, Ruth.

Rosenberg lost his position at Signal Corps in early 1945, for alleged (supposed) communist activities. Later that year, he took a job with Emerson Radio—and was soon laid off. Next, he attempted to start a non-union machine-shop business in Manhattan with his brother-in-law, David Greenglass. The business failed and both partners lost money.

In the mean time, Rosenberg had severed contacts with the Communist Party and stopped subscribing to the *Daily Worker,* a party publication. But he did not abandon his communist activities. In 1943, Rosenberg had been recruited by Aleksander Feklisov, a KGB (Soviet intelligence) officer, to spy for the Soviet Union. He began by stealing manuals for radar tubes and proximity fuses (a device that substantially increases the ability of air force fighters to shoot down enemy planes), and by the late 1940s, had two apartments set up as microfilm laboratories. He had become the coordinator of a large spy network involved in atomic, industrial, and military espionage.

A JELL-O BOX TOP

Greenglass was stationed as an assistant foreman at a machine shop in Los Alamos, New Mexico, where the lens mechanism for the atomic bomb (A-bomb) was developed. While Greenglass was on leave from his duties in Los Alamos, the Rosenbergs reportedly convinced him to provide them with secret drawings. The materials were to be passed to a spy in Los Alamos.

Later, Rosenberg gave Ruth Greenglass the torn half of a Jell-O box top, with instructions to deliver it to her husband in Los Alamos. In June 1945, a man visited Ruth and David Greenglass at their home in Los Alamos. He presented the second half of the Jell-O box top and said that he came from Julius. That man was Harry Gold, a Swiss immigrant who worked in Philadelphia, Pennsylvania, as a chemist.

In August 1949, American officials were stunned to learn that the Soviets had tested an atomic bomb. The A-bomb, which had been developed by scientists in the United States, was considered to be a national secret. The news that the Soviets had developed their own atomic weapon caused American officials to suspect an intelligence leak. It appeared that the Soviets had been able to create an atomic weapon ahead of schedule because they had obtained secret information about the U.S. atomic project.

THE DOMINO EFFECT

The U.S. government immediately set out to find the source of leaked information. A network of espionage soon came to light. First, Russian defector Igor Gouzenko informed British intelligence of the activities of a German-born scientist named Klaus Fuchs. A high-level atomic scientist on the Manhattan Project (the code name for the project to develop an atomic bomb), Fuchs had passed atomic secrets to the Soviets. In February 1950, Fuchs was arrested in England. He confessed after Soviet messages that implicated (involved) him were decoded. Partly due to Fuchs's confession, Harry Gold was arrested the following May. He admitted to receiving atomic data, which he passed to a Russian contact. He also identified the source of that information as David Greenglass

On June 15, 1950, Greenglass confessed to the Federal Bureau of Investigation (FBI) that he had passed information about the atomic bomb project to Harry Gold. He also claimed that he had handed over documents to his twenty-six-year-old sister, Ethel, and her husband, Julius. The next day FBI agents showed up at the Rosenbergs' apartment.

The Rosenbergs were listening to a radio broadcast of the *Lone Ranger* with their two young sons, Michael and Robert, when someone knocked on the door to their Manhattan apartment. Twelve FBI agents entered the apartment and arrested Julius Rosenberg as a spy. Unlike Fuchs, Gold, and Greenglass,

The world protests

The Rosenbergs' death sentence caused world-wide controversy. Scientist Albert Einstein and French president Vincent Auriol were among those who publicly urged the United States government to offer the couple clemency (mercy). After the Rosenbergs were put to death, French novelist Jean-Paul Sartre, a Nobel prize winner, called the case "A legal lynching which smears with blood a whole nation." In a form of protest, Spanish artist Pablo Picasso drew a sketch of the couple sitting in a pair of electric chairs holding hands.

Agent Gold

Harry Gold was born in Berne, Switzerland, to Russian parents. As a child, he moved to the United States with his family. The family, whose name was Golodnotzky, took the more American-sounding name of Gold. In the U.S., Harry Gold received a college education and technical training. A communist sympathizer, he was recruited by agents from the Soviet Union in 1935. Gold agreed to work as a Soviet spy and eventually specialized in stealing industrial chemical secrets. Gold was chosen by his Soviet superior, Anatoli Yakovlev, to act as a courier (a person who transports goods) for Klaus Fuchs. Fuchs provided vital information about atomic bomb preparations in the U.S. After Fuchs named Gold as a go-between, Gold was arrested. Tried for conspiracy, he was sentenced to thirty years' imprisonment.

Rosenberg protested that he was innocent. He told reporters that the FBI's story was "fantastic—something like kids hear on the *Lone Ranger* program."

THE NOOSE TIGHTENS

Rosenberg told the agents that his brother-in-law was a liar. His refusal to cooperate convinced the FBI that he was hiding something and that they were about to uncover an important spy ring. Intensifying and broadening its investigation, the FBI found Max Elitcher, who told agents that Rosenberg had approached him various times during the mid-1940s, attempting to obtain classified information that Elitcher had access to through his work with air force and navy contracts. The FBI felt it now had its case.

Ethel Rosenberg was called to appear before a grand jury (a group of people that decide if enough evidence exists to warrant a trial) on August 2, 1950. Nine days later she was called to appear again. She was arrested and sent to the Women's House of Detention in New York City. On August 17, 1950, a federal grand jury formally charged the Rosenbergs with conspiracy to commit espionage. Lack of direct evidence kept them from being charged with the more serious crime, treason. Their trial began on March 6, 1951. Morton Sobell, a former college classmate of Rosenberg's who had been implicated by Elitcher as an accomplice (someone who assists in a criminal act), was the third defendant.

A QUESTIONABLE TRIAL

From the start, the trial attracted national attention. Prosecutor Irving Saypol and his assistant, Roy Cohn, decided to keep the scope of the trial as narrow as possible. They set out to simply establish the Rosenbergs' guilt. Exposing their spy ring was a lesser concern. Even so, the trial was punctuated by numerous arrests of spies associated with the Rosenbergs, some of whom appeared in court to testify against them.

Unfair publicity and questionable procedures by Saypol jeopardized the fairness of the trial. Saypol told the jury that "the evidence of the treasonable acts of these three defendants you will find overwhelming"— even though the defendants were not accused of treason. During the trial, Saypol announced in a national news conference that he had secured sworn affidavits (statements) from an old friend of the Rosenbergs, William Perl, which proved the conspiracy beyond any doubt. Saypol decided against putting Perl on the stand, however, when Perl admitted to lying in his affidavits.

GUILTY!

One by one, Greenglass, his wife, Gold, and Elitcher took the stand and testified that the Rosenbergs were involved in a spy ring. Although Elitcher admitted that he never actually passed any documents to Julius Rosenberg, Greenglass damaged the Rosenbergs by testifying that Julius had arranged for him to give Gold the design of an atomic bomb. When Gold testified, he named Anatoli Yakovlev as his contact. This directly tied the Rosenbergs to a known Soviet agent.

The Rosenbergs denied any wrongdoing on their part. When Saypol questioned them about their past association with the Communist Party, they pleaded the Fifth Amendment and refused to answer. (The Fifth Amendment prevents an individual from being forced to offer testimony that may prove his or her guilt in a crime.)

Sobell never took the stand. A large part of Saypol's case rested on Sobell's flight to Mexico and Julius Rosenberg's attempt to obtain a passport after Fuch's confession. The defendants' attempted flight made them appear guilty in the eyes of the jury. After about eighteen hours of deliberating (deciding innocence or guilt), the jury found all three defendants guilty of conspiracy.

"WORSE THAN MURDER"

Judge Irving Kaufman had the responsibility of sentencing the Rosenbergs. Although the defendants had not been convicted of treason, the judge appeared to pass sentence on unproven acts and an uncharged crime. Announcing that the crime was "worse than murder," he explained that "putting into the hands of the Russians the A-bomb has already caused, in my opinion, the communist aggression in Korea, with its resultant casualties exceeding fifty thousand and who knows but what that millions more innocent people may pay the price of your treason." (The Korean War, 1950–1953, was a conflict between communist and non-communist powers.) The Espionage Act of 1917 gave the judge the power to impose the death sentence. On April 5, 1951, Kaufman sentenced the Rosenbergs to die in the electric chair— a sentence more fitting a treason conviction than the lesser charge of espionage. Sobell received a sentence of thirty years in prison.

INTERNATIONAL PROTESTS

The Rosenbergs unsuccessfully appealed their convictions for two years, eventually taking their case to the U.S. Supreme Court. Meanwhile, the public interest in their case reached international proportions. Many people protested the hysteria (excessive panic) of the trial and the extreme harshness of the punishment. Demonstrators urged the government to commute (to reduce it to a lesser sentence) the Rosenbergs' death sentence. Supreme Court justice William O. Douglas, issued a temporary stay (postponement) of execution.

Some supporters were against the idea of executing a woman. Others maintained that Ethel, who knew of her husband's work, but was not directly responsible for espionage, had been condemned to death as a means to pressure Julius to reveal the identities of other spies. Some protesters believed

that the Rosenbergs had been falsely accused by Greenglass and then framed by the government. Many felt the Rosenbergs were being persecuted (unfairly harassed) because they were Jewish (although both the prosecuting attorney and the judge were Jewish).

The Rosenbergs were held in Sing Sing prison in New York for two years. The institution's only woman prisoner, Ethel was kept in what amounted to solitary confinement throughout her imprisonment. The couple were allowed one weekly visit with each another—with a wire screen between them. On June 16, 1953, Ethel wrote to President Dwight D. Eisenhower asking him to grant them their lives. She addressed him as an "affectionate grandfather," "sensitive artist," and "devoutly religious man."

February 23, 1953. Police watch to see that there is no clash between protesters seeking clemency for the Rosenbergs (left) and those picketers, like the man in front, who favor their executions.

Executed for espionage

Ethel and Julius Rosenberg were the first Americans to be executed for espionage. Ethel was the second woman in the history of the United States to be put to death. A woman named Mary Surratt, who had been involved in the assassination of President Abraham Lincoln, was the first American woman to be executed.

Ethel's pleas fell on deaf ears. Eisenhower maintained that reducing their sentences would only encourage future spies. On June 18, 1953, there were demonstrations in support of the couple in Paris, France, and New York City. The following evening, shortly before 8:00 P.M., the Rosenbergs were electrocuted in Sing Sing prison. Both died refusing to confess. In one of the many letters Ethel Rosenberg wrote in prison, she told her sons, "Always remember that we were innocent and could not wrong our conscience." Recent studies of the Rosenbergs' activities, however, show that the evidence against them was overwhelming.

Sources for Further Reading

Arms, Thomas S. *Encyclopedia of the Cold War.* New York: Facts on File, 1994, p. 491.

Cohen, Jacob. "The Rosenberg File: What Do We Really Know about the Rosenbergs and the Case Against Them?" *National Review* (July 19, 1993), p. 48+.

"Espionage." *Time* (July 31, 1950), pp. 12–13.

Gertz, Bill. "Early Cold War Spies Exposed." *Insight on the News* (August 7, 1995), p. 35.

Nash, Jay Robert. *Spies: A Narrative Encyclopedia of Dirty Deeds and Double Dealing from Biblical Times to Today.* New York: M. Evans, 1997, pp. 428–430.

Radosh, Ronald. "Final Verdict: The KGB Convicts the Rosenbergs." *The New Republic* (April 7, 1997), pp. 12–13.

Radosh, Ronald. "The Venona Files." *The New Republic* (August 7, 1995), p. 25+.

Seth, Ronald. *Encyclopedia of Espionage.* London England: New English Library, 1975, pp. 597–599.

Sicherman, Barbara, Carol Hurd Green, et al., eds. *Notable American Women: The Modern Period* Cambridge, MA: Belknap Press. 1980, pp. 601–604.

Elizabeth Van Lew

Born: October 17, 1818
Died: September 25, 1900

During the Civil War, Elizabeth Van Lew lived in the heart of the Confederacy (southern states that supported slavery). A Northerner by birth, however, she was sympathetic with the Union (northern states that opposed slavery) cause. Spying for the Northern army, she became one of the Union's most valuable sources of military intelligence.

OPPOSED TO SLAVERY

The Van Lews were a prominent Virginia family. Elizabeth's father, a native of Jamaica, New York, had moved to Richmond to start a hardware business. During a trip to Philadelphia, Pennsylvania, he met a woman named Elizabeth Baker—the daughter of Hillary Baker, the city's former mayor. The couple returned to Richmond, where they were married in St. John's Church. Some time after Elizabeth was born, the Van Lews had a son, John.

As a young girl, Van Lew led a privileged existence that included tutors, dance instructors, music teachers, and riding lessons. She was sent to private school in Philadelphia, Pennsylvania, where she lived with her mother's family. At a time when Northern and Southern states were increasingly divided over the question of slavery, the Southern-born Van Lew was exposed to an environment where slavery was openly condemned. After she returned home from Philadelphia, she convinced her father to free the family's fifteen slaves. And she did

"For four years she was the sole representative of the power of the United States Government behind Rebel [Confederate] lines," said General George Henry Sharpe—chief of the U.S. Army's Bureau of Military Intelligence. But to the members of the community where she lived, she was nothing more than a traitor.

not stop there. She convinced her family to purchase other slaves in order to free them. Van Lew sent one of the former slaves—Mary Elizabeth Bowser—to school in Philadelphia.

LIFE IN CHURCH HILL

The Van Lews lived in a large white mansion, in an area of Richmond known as Church Hill. The family entertained Richmond society at their home—hosting garden parties in the terraced gardens, horseback rides in the country, and elaborate formal balls. They received many prominent guests, including poet and short story writer Edgar Allen Poe, who read his eerie poem, "The Raven," aloud in the family's library.

Sometime around 1855, Van Lew's brother, John married. When their father died in 1860, he left behind a substantial fortune. John took over the family's hardware business, and Van Lew, who never married, continued to live at the family's mansion with her mother and a number of servants.

CIVIL WAR

On April 12, 1861, the conflict between Northern and Southern states erupted into civil war. While their neighbors wholeheartedly embraced the Confederate cause, the Van Lews openly stated that they supported the Northern abolitionists who fought to do away with slavery. (The eleven states of the Confederacy wanted to secede, or withdraw, from the Union.) It was a daring move. Because of their beliefs, Van Lew and her mother were outcasts in their community. They were shunned on the street and publicly ridiculed. Accused of being traitors, they received threats against their lives. Threatening messages were posted on the front door of their house, and they were warned that their home would be set on fire during the night.

In spite of resistance from Confederate officials, Van Lew received permission to visit jails where Northern soldiers were imprisoned. A pass allowed her to visit prisoners and to bring them books to cheer them up, clothing, and food to supplement their meager diets. She also tended to sick prisoners—one of whom later remembered that she had given him grapes to eat when he was burning with a fever. During the four years of the Civil War, Van Lew visited Northern soldiers at the Confederate prisons of Belle Isle, Castle Goodwin, Castle Thunder, and Libby Prison. At some point during that time, she became a spy for the North.

A UNION SPY

Because she was able to travel freely through Confederate prisons, Van Lew had access to inside information about the Southern war effort. The information she received came from a number of sources. Northern soldiers gathered valuable information about the enemy's troops as they were transported to prison. They saw where the troops were positioned—and they counted men, horses, and weapons. They also took into account the soldiers' state of mind—something that could affect their performance on the battlefield. In prison, the soldiers counted horses, men, cannons and weapons that left for battle. And they listened to prison guards who let slip details about Confederate battle plans—sometimes even baiting their captors into providing information about enemy troops. All this information was passed to Van Lew, who, as far as the prison guards were concerned, was nothing more than a harmless woman who sympathized with the Northerners.

But Van Lew was far from harmless to the Confederate cause. After collecting vital military intelligence from Northern prisoners, she relayed the information—in coded reports—to Union officers in the North. She accomplished this by forwarding messages through a network of five posts—the first of which was the Van Lew family's mansion on Church Hill in Richmond. To relay messages she used a number of spies, including servants who carried messages in their shoes. Some reports were hidden in baskets of fruit or eggs that were carried by servants from one location to another. Others were sewn into clothing by a dressmaker who worked for Van Lew. Conveyed through common daily activities, Van Lew's messages reportedly reached

Don't judge a book by its cover

The Van Lew home contained an enormous library filled with books. When she visited imprisoned Union soldiers, she often brought bags full of books for them to read. But the books did not simply help the prisoners pass time. After Van Lew returned home with books she had lent to prisoners, she carefully examined them. Often she found marks over letters and lightly underlined words. After she pieced together the messages, she compiled reports which she forwarded to Union officers.

Secret code and invisible ink

Van Lew knew better than to attempt to pass information to Northern leaders herself. She used a network of spies—many of whom were loyal servants who relayed information during their daily routines. But not all her spies were in her employ. An unknown associate described how she relayed some of her messages through enemy lines:

She had many ways of sending this information through the Rebel lines; sometimes she would send it by persons who were comparative strangers to her. In that case, she wrote out her cipher [code] in invisible ink, a liquid which looked like water and could be brought out by milk and heat.

(The unsigned note was found among Van Lew's papers, which have been preserved. It was written in pencil on a piece of ledger paper—in handwriting that is not Van Lew's.)

Northern leaders within twenty-four hours.

ESCAPED PRISONERS

Van Lew did not limit her activities to spying for the North. Appalled by the conditions that the Union prisoners lived, she helped soldiers who escaped by hiding them in the secret room in the family's mansion.

In January 1864, Van Lew learned that all Union prisoners in Richmond were scheduled to be relocated to Andersonville—a hellish prison further south, in Georgia. On January 30—using her code name, "Mr. Babcock"—Van Lew relayed the following message to Brigadier General Ben Butler:

It is intended to remove to Georgia very soon, all the Federal [Union] prisoners; butchers and bakers to go at once. They are already notified and selected. Quaker [one of Van Lew's spies] knows this to be true. . . . Beware of rash [hasty] councils. This I send to you by direction of all your friends. No attempt should be made with less than 30,000 cavalry [soldiers on horseback], with 10,000 to 15,000 infantry [foot soldiers] to support them, amounting to all 40,000 or 45,000 troops. Do not underrate their strength or desperation.

The following month, Union soldiers organized a raid to free Union soldiers imprisoned in Richmond. One unit was organized to liberate the prisoners at Belle Isle. The unit was led by twenty-one-year-old Colonel Ulric Dahlgren—the youngest colonel in the Union army. But as Dahlgren's men approached Richmond, they were encircled by Confederate troops. The young colonel was killed and the raiding party destroyed.

Outlaws, Mobsters & Crooks

Van Lew did not abandon her efforts to help imprisoned Union soldiers. In the winter of 1864, one hundred and nine Union inmates escaped from Libby Prison by burrowing through a fifty-eight-foot tunnel. Union officers credited Van Lew with planning and assisting the escape. The Richmond newspapers also blamed Van Lew for the daring escape. One newspaper, the Richmond *Times Dispatch,* published the following account of Van Lew's role:

> Following Miss Van Lew's instructions, the fugitives, led by Colonel Streight [Colonel Abel Streight, a Union officer], scurried to a number of unfrequented spots about the closely guarded city, where her agents met them and placed them in temporary shelters, providing them with clothes—farmers, laborers, civilians and women. When their escape was discovered alarm guns were sounded and churchbells rung. Many were quickly recaptured but those who followed her [Van Lew's] instructions, safely passed through the lines. . . .

Union general Ulysses S. Grant.

STARS AND STRIPES FOREVER

By April 1865, it was clear that the South was losing the war. Confederate troops retreated to Richmond from territories that had been taken over by Union soldiers. Amid rumors that the city would be evacuated (cleared of people), the residents of Richmond watched helplessly as the city fell into riot. Mobs overwhelmed the city's police, looting stores and setting fires. Van Lew wrote in her diary:

> The city was burning. Our beautiful flour mills, the largest in the world and the prize of our city, were destroyed. Square after square of stores, dwelling homes, factories, warehouses, banks, hotels, bridges, all wrapped in fire—all filled the city with clouds of smoke as incense from the land for its

deliverance. What a moment. Avenging wrath appeased in flames!

As Richmond burned, Van Lew raised a twenty-by-nine-foot flag from her home on Church Hill. It was the Union flag—whose thirty-four stars represented the states of the Union *including* the eleven states of the Confederacy. It was the first such flag to be raised in Richmond since 1861. Hours later, the city surrendered to Union commander Ulysses S. Grant (1822–1885). The war was over on April 9, 1865, when the Confederate States of America formally surrendered. The last of the Confederate troops surrendered at Shreveport, Louisiana.

AN OUTCAST

Grant became president in 1869. Fifteen days after his inauguration, his first official act was to appoint Van Lew as postmaster of Richmond. Van Lew, who had spent her family's fortune in her wartime efforts, was awarded a yearly salary of $4,000. But the appointment did not change the way the people of Richmond felt toward Van Lew. She continued to be treated as a traitor. When Grant's term in office ended, she lost the postmastership—and the small salary she depended on. Eventually she was forced to accept a small pension from the family of one of the Union soldiers she had helped during the war.

Having outlived her mother, brother, and even her two nieces, Van Lew died on September 25, 1900, at the age of seventy-two. She was buried two days later at the family plot in Shockhoe Cemetery. Two years later, a 2,000-pound grave marker arrived at the cemetery. In the center was an inscription that read:

Elizabeth Van Lew

1818–1900

She risked everything that is dear to man—friends, fortune, comfort, health, life itself, all for the one absorbing desire of her heart, that slavery be abolished and the Union be preserved.

This Boulder From the Capitol Hill in Boston, is a tribute from her Massachusetts friends.

Sources for Further Reading

Horan, James. *Desperate Women.* New York: Putnam, 1952, pp. 125–168.

Kulkan, Mary-Ellen. *Her Way: Biographies of Women for Young People.* Chicago: American Library Association, 1976, p. 289.

Seth, Ronald. *Encyclopedia of Espionage.* London, England: New English Library, 1975, pp. 358–360.

Umlauf, Hana. *The Goodhousekeeping Woman's Almanac.* New York: Newspaper Enterprise Association, 1977, p. 455.

Swindlers

*W*ebster's Unabridged Dictionary (10th ed.) defines the verb *swindle*: "to obtain money or property by fraud or deceit." In short, swindlers practice the fine art of fooling people — for personal gain. Why did Clifford Irving write a phony biography of reclusive billionaire Howard Hughes? What made Cassie Chadwick pretend that she was the illegitimate daughter of steel magnate Andrew Carnegie? What made Joseph "Yellow Kid" Weil hire actors to pose as bank employees? The answer to each of these questions is simple: they did it for the money—and maybe, just a little, for the thrill of it. Meet the swindlers who perpetrated hoaxes, set scams in motion, and otherwise bilked their victims out of money, property—and in some cases, pride.

Cattle Kate
(Ella Watson)

Born: c. 1861
Died: 1888
AKA: Kate Maxwell

Caught in the battles between cattle barons and small ranchers, Ella Watson was a cattle rustler who paid for her thefts with her life.

HEADING WEST

The oldest of ten children, Watson was born in Lebanon, Kansas. Her father was a wealthy farmer. When she was about sixteen years old, Watson ran away to join the carnival in St. Louis, Missouri. When the family found her, she was forced to return to Lebanon. At the age of eighteen she married a middle-aged widower, who was also a farmer. Less than two years later, she left her husband, who had been unfaithful.

Watson headed for Kansas City, Missouri, where she worked as a maid for a prominent banker. After a brief stay there, she left Missouri for Red Cloud, Nebraska, where she worked as a dancer and saloon hostess. After about one year in Red Cloud, she headed for Denver, Colorado, where she spent several months. Next she headed to Wyoming, where she worked for a while in a Cheyenne dance hall. She finally landed in Rawlins, Wyoming—in the middle of cattle country.

A dark devil in the saddle

When Ella Watson arrived in Sweetwater Valley in the Wyoming Territory, cowboys and ranchers outnumbered the area's women residents. A few months after she arrived in the valley, the *Cheyenne Mail Leader* published a disapproving description of the unconventional woman known as "Cattle Kate:"

She was one of the most unforgettable women on the range. She was of robust [strong] physique, a dark devil in the saddle, handy with a six shooter and a Winchester [rifle], and an expert with the branding iron and lariat [rope]. Where she came from no one knows, but all agree, she was a holy terror. She rode straddle [not side-saddle, as women of that era were expected to], always had a vicious bronc[o] [wild horse] for a mount, and seemed never to tire of dashing across the range . . . .

THE BIG PLAINS OF WYOMING

The territory of Wyoming was created in 1868 out of sections of the Dakota, Idaho, Oregon, and Utah territories. The name "Wyoming" came from a Delaware Indian expression meaning "at the big plains." The plains (grasslands) of Wyoming provided ideal conditions for raising cattle, which were left to roam on open ranges.

The Homestead Act, enacted in 1860, was meant to bring settlers into the area. Under the Act, individuals were permitted to claim up to 160 acres of public land. After working the land for five years, they could register the land and claim the title (proof of ownership). If a man wanted to claim ownership in less than five years, he was required to work the land for six months. At the end of that time, he was offered the option to purchase the claim at the cost of $1.25 per acre.

MOUNTING TENSION

Because Wyoming was ideally suited to raising cattle, the Homestead Act was abused by greedy cattle barons (cattle ranchers that controlled large areas of land). Staking illegal claims, they established enormous ranches in the area. They claimed vast areas of government land, making it very difficult for individual homesteaders to stake their claims—and even more difficult for them to raise cattle. Many of the cattle barons were absentee land owners who rarely—if ever—showed up to survey their claims. Some were the heirs (recipients) of English fortunes, such as the Powder River Land and Cattle Company, which controlled 100,000 acres and 50,000 head of cattle. The Scottish-owned Swan Company consisted of 500,000 acres of land and more than 100,000 cattle. Independent ranchers, on the other hand, owned only a couple of hundred head of cattle.

The large cattle empires and small homesteaders soon became rivals. They clashed over land and water use, and each accused the other of stealing livestock. Many of the large ranches freely plundered the settlers' herds. With the assistance of the Wyoming Stock Growers' Association—a collection of wealthy cattle men and powerful politicians—the ranchers passed the "Maverick Law." The law enabled members of the association to claim any unbranded calf that was found on his property. But the association offered an unusual definition of "unbranded" stock. Any calf that did not have the brand of one of the cattle outfits in the Stock Growers' Association was considered to be unbranded— even if it was marked with the brand of an independent owner. The Maverick Law gave association members the right to claim a small rancher's herd as property of the association.

Many of the small herd owners responded by stealing cattle from the large cattle outfits who, in their view, had stolen government lands. They then rebranded the cattle, and claimed them as their own. Angered by their losses, the cattle barons hired detectives to spy on the small ranchers—and to catch rustlers.

Handy with a gun and iron

Stolen cattle were kept in the corral next to Cattle Kate's cabin. She was said to be handy with a gun and a branding iron, and took an active role in the rustling.

CATTLE KATE'S CORRAL

Somewhere around the time of Watson's arrival in Johnson County, a general store and saloon owner named James Averill had begun to speak out against the cattle barons. In letters to the editor of the *Casper Weekly Mail,* he called them "land-grabbers" and "land mad men." He complained that there were "four men alone claiming the Sweetwater [a river in Sweetwater Valley] seventy-five miles from its mouth [where a river begins]." He urged lawmakers to alter the area's irrigation (watering system) so that farms would thrive. In short, Averill became the hero of the independent ranchers—and the enemy of the cattle empires.

Shortly after Averill became the unofficial leader of the smaller ranchers, he met Watson at a saloon in Rawlins, and

The Johnson County War

The lynching of James Averill and Ella Watson—and the local government's failure to punish their killers—divided the residents of Johnson County. Those who sympathized with the large cattle barons felt that the vigilantes deserved to have been set free. Independent ranch owners, on the other hand, felt that Averill and Watson were innocent victims whose killers had gone unpunished.

After the six vigilantes were acquitted of the double hanging, the area's small independent ranchers increased their efforts to rustle cattle from the stockgrowers' empire. And the large cattle barons, in turn, continued to seize cattle from the independent ranchers. Tensions mounted until April 1892, when forty-one vigilantes—who called themselves "Regulators"—spread through Johnson County on a mission to kill many of the area's rustlers. Made up of Wyoming cattlemen and their detectives, the Regulators also included twenty-one Texas gunmen who had been hired to break-up the independent ranchers.

The Regulators killed two known rustlers, Nick Ray and Nate Champion. A third man escaped and informed William "Red" Angus, the Johnson County Sheriff. An enemy of the Stock Growers' Association, Angus had been elected by the area's numerous independent ranchers. On April 10, Sheriff Angus and some three hundred men headed to the TA Ranch, where the Regulators were hiding. A shoot-out followed, but to little effect. On April 13, the battle ended suddenly when U.S. Cavalry troops arrived from Fort McKinney. After a ceasefire (when both sides agree to stop fighting) was arranged, the Regulators surrendered. Of the forty-six Regulators only one was killed and none were punished for the deaths of Champion and Ray.

asked her to travel with him to Sweetwater Valley. He set her up on a homestead (working farm) within one mile of his saloon and hired workers to build a single-story log cabin on the property. He also sent a fourteen-year-old boy named Gene Crowder to help her take care of a couple of cows. Once Watson was established, he sent men who frequented his saloon to visit her. Watson's home soon became the site of an illegal business. Working as a prostitute, she sometimes received livestock as payment, for which she became known as "Cattle Kate."

Many of the animals Watson received had been stolen from the herds of the cattle barons. What's more, by the spring of 1889, Averill had organized a group of men to roundup the mavericks in the large ranchers' herds. The stolen cattle were then branded with Watson's mark and kept in her corral. Next, they were driven to a ranch used by rustlers and then to the railroad, where they were boarded onto trains to be shipped to slaughterhouses in the Midwest. The plan seemed to be foolproof. If the ranchers found Watson with stolen cattle in her corral, she could claim that she had received them as payment—and that she had nothing to do with their theft.

SOMETHING AWFUL

Angered by the repeated thefts, members of the Stock Growers' Association took the law into their own hands. On July 20, 1889, a powerful rancher named Albert J. Bothwell organized a group of association members to put a stop to Watson and Averill's rustling. Having lost a battle with Averill over his right to fence off government land, Bothwell had become the rustlers' most recent target. Adding to his desire to put Averill and Watson out of business was the fact that their homesteads were on land that Bothwell had claimed illegally.

A group of vigilantes (self-appointed doers of justice) kidnapped Averill and Watson and headed for a canyon about four miles from Watson's cabin. Averill's foreman, Jim Buchanan, had seen the kidnapping, and followed them to the south bank of the Sweetwater River. The two captives, who had been ordered to stand on boulders in the rock-strewn gully, seemed to take the kidnapping lightly. They reportedly insulted the ranchers and laughed at their threats.

Buchanan fired on the vigilantes. Outnumbered, he managed only to anger the men further. Tying a noose around the necks of their two victims, the vigilantes hanged Averill and Watson from the branch of a cottonwood tree. Buchanan had witnessed the lynchings from his hiding place and later described the scene:

> The murderers divided into two groups. Each group took the other end of the lasso and slowly pulled Jim and Kate into the air. Their necks weren't broken by a fall. They were strangled. Kate was the worst and took the longest. She kicked so hard her beaded moc-

Don't fence me in

The Wyoming Stock Growers' Association had political ties that helped pass laws in their favor. One such law allowed them to fence in government-owned land. The same law made it illegal for a rancher who was not a member of the association to cut the fence.

casins flew through the air. . . . She struggled for about fifteen minutes before she became dead. After she died, I looked at Jim and he was already dead.

The *Casper Weekly Mail*—which had once printed Averill's complaints against the ranchers—reported the hangings: "A point overlooked by the amateur executioners was tying the limbs of their victims. The kicking and the writhing of these two people was something awful. . . ."

THE CORONER'S VERDICT

Buchanan eventually found his way to a ranch, where he reported the lynchings. (He later claimed to have gotten lost on his way back from the site of the murders, but some historians think it is more likely that he had taken time to decide whether he should risk his own life by reporting the incident.) The rancher then rode fifty miles to the town of Casper to summon the sheriff. On his way there, he informed several ranchers of the double-murder.

With Buchanan to direct him, the sheriff rode with a posse (a group of people with legal authority to capture criminals) of independent ranchers to the spot where Averill and Watson had been killed. According to the *Casper Weekly Mail,* they found "the bodies swaying to and fro by the gentle breeze which wafted the sweet odor of the prairie flowers across the plains." An inquest (inquiry) into the killings was held. Based on the testimony of Buchanan, Crowder, and another employee of Averill's, the coroner's jury ruled that Averill and Watson had died by hanging—and that several ranchers, including Bothwell, were responsible. Six ranchers were charged with murder and held in the Casper jail.

The lynching party was tried in Rawlins before the town's only judge—who happened to be employed by a Cheyenne law firm responsible for handling legal matters for the Stock Growers' Association. The judge set bail for each of the defendants at $5,000. And he allowed each one to sign another's bond. In short, he allowed them to go free.

CASE DISMISSED

Bothwell and the other posse members were summoned to court on July 26. As they awaited trial before the Carbon County Grand Jury, the county coroner wrote a letter to the governor of Wyoming. He claimed that the case would not be treated fairly because the legal officials—as well as Governor Warren—were "interested parties." That is, because of their involvement with the association, they would not be capable of rendering (giving) a fair verdict. Governor Warren and the prosecutor's office insisted that the ranchers would be given a fair trial. But the coroner was suspicious of their notion of fair play. He told a reporter, "By fair trial they mean that none of the accused ever will spend a day in jail. All state officials, legislature [lawmakers], even the governor, have been corrupted by the association."

And he was probably right. Of the six defendants, only Bothwell was indicted (formally charged). The grand jury released the other vigilantes because of a lack of evidence against them. Because his bond had been paid, Bothwell remained free until his trial. By mid-December, all the prosecution witnesses disappeared. Gene Crowder was found dead, and then Jim Buchanan vanished. (Buchanan's remains—which were found near Casper four years later—were identified by a tic fastener that he always wore.) And a third witness, who had seen the kidnapping, was mysteriously shot and killed.

With no witnesses to testify against Bothwell, the case was dismissed for lack of evidence. But the double-hanging did not go unnoticed. A newspaper that supported the independent ranchers announced "If it's lynching they want, two can play the game." The small ranchers grew increasingly resentful of the cattle barons, and by April 1892, the conflict erupted into the Johnson County War. The lynching of Watson and Averill is considered to have been a major contributing factor to the tensions that sparked that war.

CHEAP LAND

Sometime after he was cleared of the murder charges, Bothwell contested (challenged) the homestead claims of Averill and

Watson. Because their taxes had not been paid, Bothwell was allowed to purchase their land for a total of $14.93. Bothwell had Watson's cabin taken apart and reassembled on his ranch, where he used it as an icehouse.

Sources for Further Reading

The American West, A Cultural Encyclopedia, Volume 5. Danbury, CT: Grolier Educational Corp., 1995, pp. 833–837.

Horan, James. *Desperate Women.* New York: G. P. Putnam's Sons, 1952, pp. 227–241.

Lamar, Howard Roberts. *The Reader's Encyclopedia of the American West.* New York: Harper & Row, 1977, p. 182.

McLoughlin, Denis. *Wild and Woolly, An Encyclopedia of the Old West.* New York: Doubleday, 1975, pp. 542–543.

Nash, Jay Robert. *Bloodletters and Badmen.* New York: M. Evans, 1973, pp. 595–596.

Ward, Geoffrey. *The West, An Illustrated History.* Boston: Little, Brown, 1996, pp. 368–370.

Cassie Chadwick
(Elizabeth Bigley)

Born: 1859
Died: October 10, 1907
AKA: Constance Cassandra Chadwick,
Cassie L. Hoover, Lydia D. Scott,
Lydia Springsteen, Lydia de Vere

As a young woman and well into middle age, Cassie Chadwick used her elegant manner and acting ability to pull off confidence schemes that earned her thousands of dollars—and a prison term.

FORGERY AND FRAUD

Chadwick was born Elizabeth Bigley, near London, Ontario, Canada. The daughter of a railway worker, she was from a poor family. Chadwick began her career as a con woman and swindler (person who cheats people out of money) when she was still in her teens. At the age of sixteen, she attempted to forge a check for $5,000. (Forgers pass off fake checks as real. Sometimes they forge, or fake, the signature of somebody else. Other times they write checks drawn on accounts that don't exist.) Caught forging the check, Chadwick was not jailed because the court found her temporarily insane.

When she was twenty-five years old, she married W. S. Springsteen, a physician. Using his name as a reference and his property as collateral (property that is pledged to protect the lender), she borrowed money. Springsteen eventually had to sell his home in order to repay Chadwick's debts. One year after they were married, the couple divorced. Chadwick then moved

Cassie Chadwick's extravagant diningroom at her home in Cleveland. Some of her silverware was studded with rubies.

to Toledo, Ohio, where she started a business as a fortune teller named Lydia de Vere. She claimed that she could make sick men healthy—and poor men wealthy. Chadwick would hire private detectives to find out what they could about her clients. Armed with embarrassing information that her clients wanted to keep secret, she collected thousands of dollars by blackmailing her victims. (Blackmail is a form of extortion in which threats are used to gain payment.) After one of her clients threatened to take her to court, Chadwick abandoned her fortune-telling scam. But she soon landed in court anyway. Caught with $20,000 in forged bills, she was convicted of fraud (deliberate deception) and forgery. Although she was sentenced to nine years in prison, she was released in 1897, after serving only three years behind bars.

THE CARNEGIE SCAM

After she was released Chadwick settled in Cleveland, Ohio, where she adopted the identity of Cassie L. Hoover, a widow. She met and married Dr. Leroy Chadwick, a wealthy and well-respected older man. After they were married, Chadwick threw lavish parties in their stylish home on Euclid Avenue. She also traveled out of town on extravagant trips.

During a trip to New York City, Chadwick set in motion an elaborate scam that involved the famous millionaire Andrew Carnegie. First, Chadwick rented expensive rooms at the exclusive Holland House. There she managed to bump into James Dillon, a Cleveland lawyer who knew her slightly. As far as Dillon knew, their meeting was accidental. But Chadwick had arranged the coincidence. She knew that Dillon was scheduled to be in New York on business and arranged her trip accordingly.

Following their "accidental" meeting, Chadwick asked Dillon to join her on an errand. At Chadwick's instruction, they rode in a coach up Fifth Avenue in a wealthy section of Manhattan. Chadwick ordered the coach to stop in front of a residence, telling the lawyer that she would only be a few minutes. Almost everyone—especially bankers and lawyers—knew that the spacious quarters belonged to the multi-millionaire Andrew Carnegie.

THE SCAM DEVELOPS

Chadwick knocked at Carnegie's door and was admitted. Posing as a wealthy New Yorker, she pretended that she wanted to check the reference of a maid who claimed to have worked for Carnegie. In order to make her story more believable, she carried a fake letter of application from the make-believe job applicant. The housekeeper informed Chadwick that no such maid had ever worked for Carnegie. When Chadwick acted puzzled, the housekeeper checked her files to find out whether the woman had ever worked at any of the millionaire's other homes. Chadwick thanked the housekeeper for her time and left.

Steel magnate

Andrew Carnegie (1835–1919) earned millions of dollars as a steel magnate (successful business person). Chadwick borrowed hundreds of thousands of dollars by pretending to be the millionaire bachelor's daughter. But Carnegie had no children. What's more, he never even met Chadwick, his supposed daughter.

Spending spree

Cassie Chadwick had no trouble spending thousands of dollars of "borrowed" money. She once reportedly purchased *twenty-seven* grand pianos on credit.

Chadwick had no interest in hiring a maid. She simply needed a legitimate reason to gain entry into Carnegie's home—with James Dillon as a witness. When she returned to the carriage, after about a half hour in the Carnegie residence, she "accidentally" dropped a piece of paper in front of the lawyer. Dillon picked up the slip of paper, which was a note promising to pay two million dollars. The note was signed by Andrew Carnegie.

Pretending to be embarrassed that Dillon had seen the promissory note (a note that promises to pay a sum of money), Chadwick "confessed" that she was Carnegie's daughter. This surprised him since Carnegie had never married and had never acknowledged having any children. Chadwick explained that the note was one of many that Carnegie had written to help support his "illegitimate daughter."

Dillon was appalled to hear that Chadwick had several promissory notes signed by Carnegie at home. He convinced her that the notes belonged in the bank, and offered to make arrangements to secure a safe deposit box at one of the banks he represented. Chadwick agreed. After she turned over the forged Carnegie notes, Dillon gave her a receipt for $7 million—without ever checking the authenticity of the notes.

A PAUPER'S END

Chadwick wasted no time using the $7 million receipt to her advantage. With the forged notes as collateral, she borrowed hundreds of thousands of dollars from a number of bankers who were eager to lend her money—for an outrageous fee. Chadwick enjoyed the high life, purchasing expensive gowns, jewelry, paintings, and tapestries (decorative wall hangings). She bought a mansion and carriages and hired servants to work for her.

Chadwick's scheme worked smoothly until she encountered Henry Newton, a Cleveland millionaire. Borrowing $500,000 from Newton, she promised to pay a high interest (a fee that increases over time) on the loan. But Newton was not as trusting as the banks had been. He demanded that Chadwick pay the interest she owed. When Chadwick informed him that she had

Criminal activities caused grief

Following Chadwick's arrest, one newspaper claimed, "The suicide of more than one man, and the impoverishment [poverty] of probably hundreds of families, may be laid at her door."

tens of thousands of dollars worth of promissory notes in the bank, he demanded to see them. The notes—which had never been examined by any of the bankers—were soon discovered to be forgeries. And Andrew Carnegie offered no support. He denied ever having fathered a child and stated "I have never heard of Mrs. Chadwick!"

On December 7, 1904, Chadwick was arrested in the Holland House in New York—where she had first set the scam in motion. She was wearing a money belt stuffed with more than $100,000. Guards escorted her on a train back to Cleveland where she stood trial in March of the following year. She protested that she was an innocent victim who was being persecuted because she was a member of the upper class. But the prosecutor informed the court that Chadwick had a long history of forgeries, frauds, and arrests.

Take a look at this!

Set in New York in the 1980s, *Six Degrees of Separation* (1993) is based on the true story of a young man who claims to be the son of Sidney Poitier, a famous actor. Posing as the young Poitier, David Hampton (played by Will Smith) hustles his way into the lives of a number of wealthy Manhattan couples.

THE END OF A LIFE OF CRIME

The trial was brief. Convicted of six charges of fraud, Chadwick was sentenced to ten years in the Ohio State Penitentiary in Columbus. Dr. Chadwick had his marriage annulled (declared invalid) and moved to Florida. After two and a half years in prison, Cassie died in the penitentiary hospital at the age of forty-eight. Although she was scheduled to be buried in a pauper's (poor person's) grave, an unidentified man reportedly paid to have her body shipped to Canada to be buried.

Sources for Further Reading

De Grave, Kathleen. *Swindler, Spy, Rebel.* Columbia: University of Missouri Press, 1995, pp. 57–73, 144–157.

Dressler, David. "Cleveland's Queen of Society Swindlers." *Coronet* (May 1950), pp. 71–74.

Nash, Jay Robert. *The Encyclopedia of World Crime.* Wilmette, IL: Crime Books, 1990, p. 1506.

Stein, Gordon. *Encyclopedia of Hoaxes.* Detroit: Gale Research, 1993, pp. 33–34.

D. B. Cooper

Active: November 24, 1971

The identity of a man referred to as "D. B. Cooper" has never been discovered. No one knows who he was or what became of him. But on November 24, 1971, he stepped out of a plane and into history as the only hijacker in the United States to escape capture.

THE PASSENGER IN SEAT 15D

On the day before Thanksgiving in 1971, a man who identified himself as Dan Cooper (a journalist erred in reporting his name as "D. B.," and it was never cleared up) was one of thirty-six passengers who boarded Northwest Airlines flight 305. The plane, a Boeing 727, was headed from Portland, Oregon, to Seattle, Washington—a flight that would normally take less than one hour. Shortly after takeoff, when the plane had climbed to thirty thousand feet, the passenger in seat 15D gave one of the two stewardesses a note. The stewardess, Florence Schaffner, did not read the note at first. But the passenger, a middle-aged man who wore a business suit and dark glasses, insisted that she read it.

The hand-written message on the note indicated that the man had a bomb in his briefcase. Further, it said that if he did not receive $200,000 in $20 bills, along with four parachutes, he would blow up the aircraft. When pilot William Scott spoke to the man, he was convinced that the hijacker was serious.

The hijacker's demands

The crew contacted Seattle Airport Traffic Control, who in turn contacted the Seattle police. Next the Federal Bureau of Investigation (FBI) was alerted. Soon, the airplane was pursued by two F-106 fighter planes that departed from nearby McChord Air Force Base, and a National Guard helicopter that was flown by Ralph Himmelsbach, a Portland FBI agent and former World War II fighter pilot.

Cooper's conditions made sure that law enforcement authorities did not have time to devise traps. He insisted that the money and parachutes be delivered to Seattle Airport before the plane landed. With only a limited amount of fuel, the plane could not circle the airport indefinitely. This lack of time prevented FBI agents from marking the money so that it could be identified when the hijacker spent it. And by asking for four parachutes, Cooper led authorities to believe that he might not jump alone. They dared not boobytrap (purposely dismantle) any of the parachutes.

Flight instructions

At 5:40 P.M., after the plane had circled Seattle Airport for almost an hour, the crew was notified that the money and parachutes had arrived and that the aircraft was cleared to land. Cooper allowed all of the passengers and one stewardess to exit the plane. Still on board were one stewardess, the pilot, and two other crew members.

Cooper had the plane refueled for the next leg of its journey. It was to head south, toward Reno, Nevada. And it was to head there slowly, and at a low altitude. Cooper specified that the aircraft was to climb no higher than ten thousand feet. (Any higher would require a parachutist to jump with oxygen.) To make sure that the plane remained below the ten thousand-foot ceiling, Cooper wore an altimeter, a device that measures altitude, on his wrist. He also ordered the crew to leave the cabin unpressurized—probably as a precaution against climbing higher than the safe-jump zone.

Hijacking instructions manual

In 1971, commercial airline hijackings were unheard of in North America. None of the airlines' procedure manuals—which instructed the crew how to handle certain situations—provided any information on how to deal with a hijacking.

With no other hijacking cases to look to, the president of Northwest Airlines had to decide for himself how to handle the Cooper hijacking. His decision became the industry standard for dealing with hijackers: he gave Cooper exactly what he asked for.

Cooper insisted that the plane be flown no faster than 150 knots per hour. By limiting the speed at which the plane traveled, Cooper made sure that the aircraft would be difficult to follow. While the Boeing 727 was capable of maintaining altitude at that speed, many other planes would stall if the pilot tried to maintain such a sluggish (slow) pace. At best, pursuing planes would have to double back and forth to maintain contact with the skyjacked aircraft. Cooper also instructed the crew to leave the flaps and landing gear down. Once the aircraft reached ten thousand feet, Cooper ordered the four crew members to close themselves into the cockpit. It was the last they saw of him.

INTO THIN AIR

Sometime before Northwest flight 305 arrived in Reno, Nevada, Cooper parachuted into a storm in the cold, mountainous southwest Washington wilderness. He jumped at a high altitude into freezing rain, with winds that blew up to seventy miles per hour. No one knows what happened next. Some investigators believe Cooper did not survive the skydive. Of the two parachutes he took, one was a non-working training parachute that had been supplied by mistake. If he relied on that chute, he undoubtedly fell to his death.

And even if his parachute did work, Cooper's chances of surviving the jump would have been slim. Agent Himmelsbach—who worked the case from 1971 until he retired from the FBI in 1980—noted, "[Cooper] didn't ask for a helmet, gloves, flight jacket, jumpsuit, or boots. It was seven below zero outside, it was dark, and the plane was going 196 miles per hour." When he hit the air at that speed, Cooper probably tumbled head-over-heels. The wind resistance would have given him black eyes and his shoes were probably blown off.

What's more, the landing conditions where Cooper jumped would have scared away even the most experienced jumpers. Cooper's choice of parachutes (he left behind the two best chutes) suggests that he was a novice (beginner) skydiver. "Whatever Cooper would have hit down there, he would have hit hard," Himmelsbach said. "Even if he'd just sprained his leg it'd be a death sentence in that kind of environment."

Dead or not, Cooper was the subject of intensive manhunts. FBI agents, U.S. Air Force pilots, National Guardsmen, army

What happened?

If Cooper died in the forests of Washington, there wouldn't be much evidence. Small animals would have eaten his flesh and scattered his bones so that investigators would have had a hard time identifying his remains.

Outlaws, Mobsters & Crooks

troops, and civilian (non-military) volunteers searched the area where Cooper might have landed. They found no trace of the hijacker.

FOUND MONEY

For almost a decade, investigators found nothing to shed any light on the 1971 hijacking. But in February 1980, a young boy discovered a package containing several dozen $20 bills. The wet and shredded money—whose serial numbers were traceable to the ransom payment—was the only real clue that had appeared since Cooper jumped out of the jetliner. But it was a clue that led nowhere. Authorities searched the area for further clues. Again they found nothing.

None of the remaining $194,000 was ever found—nor have the serial numbers appeared in circulation. (If large sums of the money had been spent, banks, which keep track of the serial numbers on bills, would have records indicating that the cash was in use.) In spite of repeated intensive searches, no parachute was ever found. Although he apparently never enjoyed the money he ransomed, the man who called himself Dan Cooper remains the only U.S. hijacker who was never caught.

Part of the money that was paid to Cooper in 1971 was found near Portland, Oregon, on February 10, 1980, by eight-year-old Brian Ingram, who was on a family picnic.

Sources for Further Reading

Angeloff, Sam. "The FBI Agent Who Has Tracked D. B. Cooper for Nine Years Retires, But the Frustrating Search Goes On." *People Weekly* (March 3, 1980), pp. 45–46.

Gates, David. "D. B. Cooper, Where Are You?" *Newsweek* (December 26, 1983), p. 12.

Schroeder, Andreas. *Scams, Scandals, and Skulduggery.* Toronto, Ontario, Canada: McClelland & Stewart, 1996, pp. 178–191.

Williams, Geoff. "Have You Seen This Man?" *Entertainment Weekly* (November 24, 1995), p. 120.

Clifford Irving

Born: 1930

Formerly a minor author—who had trouble sticking to the truth—Clifford Irving convinced his publisher to hire him to write The Autobiography of Howard Hughes. *The trouble was, Howard Hughes had no involvement in his supposed memoirs. Irving faked the life story of the reclusive billionaire—and almost got away with it.*

EARLY LIFE

Born in New York City in 1930, Irving grew up on the Upper West Side of Manhattan. His father, Jay Irving, was a cartoonist who drew a comic strip called "Pottsy," a friendly, overweight policeman. Irving did not get along well with his father, who pressured his son to be successful. As a boy, Irving lived in his parents' New York apartment and attended public schools in Manhattan. His boyhood friends included William Safire, who later became a speechwriter for President Richard Nixon (1969–1974) and a prominent contributor to the *New York Times*.

Irving enrolled in New York's prestigious Cornell University in 1947, with the intention of becoming an artist. After he read some of the works of novelist Ernest Hemingway (1899–1961), however, he decided to become a writer. Having taken college courses in creative writing, Irving was awarded a one-year creative writing fellowship. He remained at Cornell for one year after receiving his bachelor's degree in 1951.

In the spring of his senior year, he married Nina Wilcox, a student. Irving soon became restless and the marriage fell apart. Traveling around the country, he took odd jobs to support himself. In Detroit, Michigan, he took a job in a machine shop. In Syracuse, New York, he worked as a door-to-door salesman for the Fuller Brush company. He traveled overseas, and even lived on a houseboat in Kashmir (a former princely state in northwest India and northeast India).

NOVELS AND WIVES

Irving's first novel, *On a Darkling Plain,* was published in 1956. Irving's first novel is considered to be largely autobiographical (based on the author's life). Completed during a visit to Ibiza (a Spanish island in the west Mediterranean Sea), *On a Darkling Plain* portrays the difficulties three school friends have adjusting to life in the United States after war. The following year, Irving published *The Losers,* a fictional story—told in the words of a cartoonist—about a businessman who becomes an artist. In 1961, he produced a western tale titled *The Valley.* During 1961 and 1962, Irving taught creative writing at an extension school of the University of California in Los Angeles. He later worked on various television projects and sold a script to the western series, *Bonanza.* In 1966, *The Thirty-Eighth Floor* appeared in bookstores. Irving's fourth novel concerned an African American's rise to the position of acting secretary-general of the United Nations.

Irving, in the meantime, met and married three other women. His second wife, Claire, died in a car crash in Monterey, California, in the late 1950s. She was eight months pregnant at the time. Next, Irving married a former fashion model named Fay Brooke. Wed in 1961, the couple had one son, Josh. Irving was anything but a model husband. He was a hard-core drinker, he had affairs with other women, and he beat his wife. Brooke and Irving divorced in 1965. Two years later he married a divorced painter named Edith. Born in Germany, she was the daughter of the owner of a clock factory. The couple had two children, Ned and Barnaby.

Until his role in the Howard Hughes scandal, Irving was best known as the author of *Fake!*—the supposed biography of a Hungarian art forger named Elmyr de Hory. Published in 1969, the novel received some favorable reviews. Others were less forgiving of the author's inability to stick to a factual account of the art forger's life. Although Irving was a friend of de Hory, he had invented much of his story.

THE HOAX TAKES SHAPE

With several books to his credit, Irving approached McGraw-Hill, his regular publisher, with the idea for another biography. The book was to be the authorized biography of billionaire Howard Hughes (1905–1976). A fiercely private and eccentric (unconventional) man, Hughes had not been photographed or interviewed since 1958. Irving's editors were intrigued.

But Irving had no intention of producing an authorized or factual work. (An authorized biography is an officially approved story of the subject's life.) First, Irving convinced the publishers that he was in contact with the billionaire. Using a piece of a Hughes letter that had been published in *Newsweek* magazine, Irving created fake letters from the billionaire to himself.

While he was in New York to attend his mother's funeral, Irving stopped at McGraw-Hill and showed them the phony material. The publisher was convinced that Hughes had agreed to supply the little-known author with the first and only authorized version of his life story—and convinced that such a book had the potential to earn a fortune. On March 23, 1971, Irving signed a contract with McGraw-Hill to write the authorized biography of Hughes. The contract provided an immediate advance of $100,000.

A WELL-RESEARCHED STORY

Next, Irving had to put together a manuscript of Hughes's "tell-all" account of his life. He needed some accurate material in order to lend credence (believability) to the story. He had to be able to duplicate Hughes's manner of speaking so that the words he attributed to the billionaire would sound authentic. And he needed to provide inside information and little-known details that would set his book apart from countless other works about the mysterious Mr. Hughes.

Working with a research assistant, Richard Suskind, Irving pieced together a plausible (believable) account of the life of Hughes. He consulted countless books and articles written by other authors and journalists. He researched his subject at the New York Public Library. He went to Washington, D.C., where he uncovered a useful file on the Hughes Aircraft Company at the Pentagon. At the Library of Congress, he found congressional testimony by Hughes, and a thesis that discussed the role of Trans World Airlines (TWA)—which was at that time a Hughes company—in the development of Ethiopian Airways. Suskind and Irving also examined the files of Time-Life publishers and the *Los Angeles Times*—as well as newspaper files in Houston, Texas, and Las Vegas, Nevada, for material concerning Hughes or his family. And they traveled to Los Angeles, California, to gather information about Hughes's Hollywood years.

STOLEN RESEARCH, PHONY INTERVIEWS, AND MAKE-BELIEVE MEETINGS

Much of Irving's inside information was derived from the research of another author, James Phelan, whose work on Hughes had not yet been published. Irving was approached by his friend, Stanley Myers, to rewrite a book on Hughes. Based on material provided by Noah Dietrich—who had been the billionaire's chief of staff for thirty-two years—the manuscript was filled with insider information not available in other sources. The original manuscript was compiled by Phelan, an experienced investigative reporter who had already written five magazine articles on Hughes. Irving informed Myers that he was not interested in the project. What he failed to tell Myers was that he planned to steal much of Phelan's material for his own book on Hughes.

Since their work was supposed to be from tapes dictated by Hughes, Suskind and Irving took turns dictating what they had learned into a tape recorder. The exercise helped Irving create the feeling of a book that had been dictated. It also allowed Irving to produce transcripts of the tapes to prove to McGraw-Hill that the conversations had taken place. The transcripts of the "interviews" produced nine hundred and fifty pages of typed material—which Irving copied and provided to his publishers. The original tapes were destroyed.

In order to make absolutely sure that his publishers were convinced that his story was authentic, Irving traveled to far-away destinations to "meet" with Hughes. He claimed that his first meeting with Hughes had taken place from high atop a mountain in Oaxaca, Mexico. He made trips to Florida, California, the Bahamas, Mexico, and Puerto Rico, and often called his editors. He even sent postcards from distant places to relatives—scribbling made-up stories about his fictitious (made-up) meetings with Hughes.

SWISS BANKS AND THE MYSTERIOUS HELGA HUGHES

Irving's original contract with McGraw-Hill provided for $500,000 in advances. Some of the money was to be paid to Irving. The rest was to be paid directly to Hughes. Within six months, Irving informed his publishers that Hughes—one of the richest men in the world—wanted more money for the book. Afraid that the duo would take the autobiography elsewhere, McGraw-Hill increased their offer to $750,000.

Irving's wife, meanwhile, had been busy taking care of finances. In Barcelona, Spain, she acquired a fake Swiss passport under the name of Helga Rosencrantz Hughes. Next she opened a bank account—under the name "H. R. Hughes"—at Credit Suisse in Zurich, Switzerland. Wearing a wig and dark glasses, she deposited 1,000 Swiss francs—equivalent to $260—on May 12, 1971. The following day—using the same Credit Suisse bank teller—she deposited a check from McGraw-Hill for $50,000. The check was made out to H. R. Hughes.

Two weeks later—after the check cleared—Edith withdrew the $50,000 from Credit Suisse. She then deposited the money in a numbered account in another Swiss bank. The Irvings had established a way to convert any money paid to Hughes by

McGraw-Hill (or other publishers involved in the deal) into their own account.

Edith repeated the procedure with two more checks from McGraw-Hill. She deposited $275,000 at Credit Suisse on September 30. On October 19, she appeared with an airline bag—and withdrew the entire amount in 1,000-franc notes. By withdrawing the money in francs rather than dollars, she avoided additional paperwork. The phony Mrs. Hughes made her final deposit—$325,000—toward the beginning of December. By the end of the month, she appeared at the bank—in wig and sunglasses—to claim the money.

A STATEMENT TO THE PRESS

On December 7, 1971, publisher McGraw-Hill announced that it would publish *The Autobiography of Howard Hughes.* The press release explained that Hughes had spent much of 1970 working on his memoirs with the help of Clifford Irving, an American writer. The two men reportedly spent one hundred work sessions together—often in parked cars.

The memoir, which was 230,000 words long, was to be published on March 27, 1972. *Life* magazine would publish three 10,000-word installments of the book, in addition to a separate article by Irving on the interviews. At a publishing party, it was announced that the Book-of-the-Month Club had agreed to feature the Irving book, and to pay a $350,000 advance for the right to do so. Dell Publishing Company bought the rights to publish the book in paperback for $400,000.

HUGHES CRIES *HOAX!*

Immediately after McGraw-Hill's press statement was released, a spokesman for Hughes rejected the book in no uncertain terms. A short time later, Frank McCulloch—the New York bureau chief of *Time* magazine and the last journalist to interview Hughes—was informed that the billionaire wanted to talk to him on the phone. McCulloch agreed.

To make sure that he was speaking to the *real* Hughes, McCulloch asked him two trick questions. Hughes answered the questions correctly. He also said that he had never met or heard of Irving—and that he was definitely not working on his memoirs with the man.

But McCulloch still was not convinced that Irving's book was a scam. He was convinced that the biography was genuine because Irving was able to quote what Hughes had said to him on the phone during their last conversation in the late 1950s. McCulloch thought that only he and Hughes knew what was said at that time. He had apparently forgotten that a transcript of the conversation had been made for the president of Time-Life, Inc. As Hughes's employee, Dietrich had seen the transcript. Irving had read about the conversation in the Dietrich-Phelan manuscript. With McCulloch's endorsement, McGraw-Hill decided to stand by the authenticity of the Irving book. And no one checked with the Swiss bank to find out if there was anything unusual about the person who made deposits—and withdrawals—from the H. R. Hughes account.

INCREASING SUSPICION

Irving passed a number of other "tests." All of the material supposedly written by Hughes was reexamined. The writings were inspected by a firm that had a reputation for being the finest handwriting experts in the United States. They compared the McGraw-Hill samples with the material written by Hughes when he was in Las Vegas, Nevada. They, too, confirmed that Hughes had written all of the McGraw-Hill material. Irving was given a last-minute lie-detector test. The results proved nothing—and the test was not repeated.

In January 1972, Irving was informed that Hughes was planning to hold a telephone news conference with seven journalists from Los Angeles. During the conference, the man who claimed to be Hughes told the journalists that he did not know Irving—and that he had never worked with him on a book. Irving responded that the voice was not that of Hughes—although it was a fairly accurate imitation of how the billionaire once sounded.

THE JIG IS UP

Irving's hoax began to collapse after Swiss authorities began to take a closer look at H. R. Hughes. They discovered

Dead men don't write

Some people believed that Howard Hughes was dead. They speculated that the "autobiography" was a hoax engineered by a group of Hughes employees to gain control of the billionaire's assets.

that "H. R. Hughes"—who opened the bank accounts and deposited the checks intended as payment to the billionaire—was not Howard Hughes. They knew that the deposits had been made by a woman—a woman who looked very much like Irving's five-foot-six, hazel-eyed, thirty-something wife. By the first week of February, Swiss authorities issued warrants for the arrest of Clifford and Edith Irving.

At first, Irving denied that he knew the woman who went under the name of Helga R. Hughes. He even threatened to bring a lawsuit against reporters who suggested that his wife was involved in a hoax. Eventually, he was forced to admit that Helga was, in fact, his wife. But he denied being involved in a hoax. He claimed that Hughes had provided Edith with the fake passport—and that he had instructed them to open the Swiss bank accounts. He also claimed that Edith had not endorsed any of the checks. She simply deposited the checks in the Swiss accounts after the billionaire had signed them.

But Irving's credibility (believability) had been destroyed. McGraw-Hill and *Life* magazine delayed publishing Irving's manuscript. Reporters continued to search for the truth. Soon after the Swiss authorities charged the Irvings, the author received a phone call from a reporter from *Time* magazine. The reporter had a copy of the Dietrich-Phelan manuscript. This time there was no way out. Irving could not deny that he had borrowed—or stolen—material from the unpublished biography.

The Truth at Last

Irving was investigated from every angle. The New York County district attorney, United States Postal Service, and the Justice Department all had him under investigation. Rumors began to circulate that Irving was about to be arrested. Finally, he confided in a friend, attorney Philip Lorber. (Irving's lawyer, Martin Ackerman, had quit shortly after the bank scam was discovered. He told his client to hire a criminal lawyer.) Irving admitted to Lorber that the biography was a hoax.

After Irving was formally charged, prosecuting attorneys offered to cut him a deal if he would plead guilty. They would not prosecute Edith, who was little more than a courier. And Suskind would be given a light sentence.

On May 21, 1989, Ray
Simpson (pictured here)
of Simpson's Auction
Galleries in Houston,
Texas, held an auction
for Howard Hughes
memorabilia, including
the original manuscript
of Irving's fake
autobiography.

JAIL TIME

On March 9, 1972, Irving was formally charged with federal conspiracy to defraud, forgery, and the use of forged instruments (documents), using the mail to defraud, and perjury (lying under oath in court). Suskind was charged only as a co-conspirator on the federal charges. In New York State court, both Irvings and Suskind were charged with grand larceny (theft), conspiracy, and a few minor charges. They pleaded guilty to all charges.

Clifford Irving was sentenced to two-and-a-half years in jail. After serving about seven months in Allenwood Federal Prison in Pennsylvania, he was paroled (released from jail before his sentence was fully served). Edith Irving was sentenced to two years—of which all but two months were suspended. Richard Suskind was sentenced to six months in prison.

The Swiss authorities at first refused to drop charges against Edith, who had used false documents to enter the country, open bank accounts, and conduct transactions. The authorities later agreed to drop the charges—and then changed their minds again. In Zurich, Edith was tried and convicted of forgery, embezzlement (taking money by illegal means), and theft. Sentenced to two years in jail, she served the entire term.

WHAT REALLY HAPPENED?

Irving's hoax biography of Hughes has never been published. But his account of his involvement in the scandal—called *What Really Happened*—was available for public consumption in 1972. (McGraw-Hill would not publish it.) A reviewer in *Time* magazine noted that it would be difficult to view Irving's work (co-authored with Suskind) as a true story. "To believe the confessions of Clifford Irving," the author writes, "is a little like believing the confessions of Baron Munchausen." (Baron Karl Friedrich Hieronymus von Munchausen was a German soldier and hunter who lived from 1720 to 1797. He was famous not for his military exploits—but for the wild lies he told about his adventures.)

Sources for Further Reading

"Clifford & Edith & Howard & Helga." *Time* (February 7, 1972), pp. 20–22.

"The Fabulous Hoax of Clifford Irving." *Time* (February 21, 1972), pp. 12–17.

Friedrich, Otto. "Caper Sauce." *Time* (September 18, 1972), pp. 92–93.

"The Great Hughes Fiasco." *Newsweek* (February 7, 1972), pp. 18, 20, 23.

"Irving's Latest Cliff-Hanger." *Newsweek* (February 14, 1972), pp. 20–22.

Nash, Jay Robert. *The Encyclopedia of World Crime.* Wilmette, IL: Crime Books, 1990, pp. 1665–1666.

Sophie Lyons

Born: December 24, 1848
Died: May 8, 1924
AKA: Fannie Owens,
Kate Wilson, Mary Wilson

*A petty (small-time) thief from the time she could walk, Sophie Lyons eventually earned
a reputation as "one of the cleverest criminals the country has ever produced."*

A CRIMINAL EDUCATION

Born Sophie Levy in New York City on December 24, 1848, she was the daughter of criminals. Her mother—who used the names Julia Keller and Sophie Elkins—was an old-time shoplifter. She saw little of her father, Sam Levy, who spent much of his life in prison for robbery. Sophie's mother taught her to shoplift at an early age. She also instructed her in the practice of picking pockets—which was considered to be an art among criminals of that time. Taught various ways to steal to help support her family, Sophie never attended school.

As a teenager Sophie married a pickpocket named Maury Harris, who was caught and jailed soon after they married. Having left her husband, she met and married Ned Lyons, a burglar and bank robber who was highly respected in the criminal community. Born in England in 1837, Ned participated in a number of successful robberies—including the theft of nearly $800,000 from the Ocean Bank in New York on June 27, 1869. He also led a group of burglars who collected $150,000 from vaults in the Philadelphia Navy Yard in 1870.

A TALENTED ACTRESS

A successful thief, Ned reportedly wanted his wife to give up crime. He bought an extravagant home on Long Island, New York. He hired servants and purchased expensive furniture, china, and other household items. Lyons no longer needed to steal to survive—but she continued to steal anyway. During one of her outings, Lyons was arrested by a detective who caught her picking pockets at a fair. The arrest report describes how Lyons's behavior at the jailhouse helped her to regain her freedom:

> She was then only nineteen years old, but her phenomenal [exceptional] talent as an actress was already developed. She could mold her face to every shade of emotion. She could make her eyes at will a fountain of tears. She treated us to a moving display of her art. She was by turns horror-stricken, proudly indignant [angered by something unjust], heartbroken, and convulsed with hysterics. Who could press a charge against such a blushing, trembling, sobbing young beauty piteously claiming that it was a dreadful mistake, painting the agony of her dear husband and parents at the bare suspicion of her spotless innocence, and subtly hinting at the grave censure [severe criticism] that would surely fall on her maligners [those who spoke ill of her]? It was her shrewd [cunning] calculation that the authorities in charge of her case would prefer to let it drop quietly, and so they did.

Lyons was set free.

ESCAPE FROM SING SING

Lyons was arrested again in early 1871 when she was caught stealing from a jewelry store in New York—for which she was sent to prison on Blackwell's Island, New York. Soon after she was released she was tried for grand larceny (theft). Con-

victed on October 9, 1871, she was sentenced to five years in Sing Sing state prison.

But prison might have been part of Lyons's master plan. At the time of her trial, Ned was serving a long sentence in Sing Sing. Many people believe that Lyons was arrested on purpose—so that she could help her husband to escape. Soon after she arrived at the prison, Lyons became a personal assistant to the matron (female supervisor) of the women's division at Sing Sing. She wore a maid's outfit instead of prison clothes, and walked freely outside of prison walls with the matron's children. Taking advantage of her freedom, she managed to have clothing, a wig, and a forged (faked) prison pass smuggled to her. Dressed in street clothes and armed with a prison pass, Ned simply walked out of jail. On December 19, 1872, Sophie also

Sing Sing prison, in Ossining, New York.

walked to freedom, using a key her husband had made from a wax impression.

But their freedom was short-lived. After a brief stay in Canada, where the couple robbed a pawnbroker (person who loans money on items left as a security deposit) of more than $40,000, both the Lyons were arrested for pickpocketing at the Suffolk County fair on Long Island. On October 26, 1876, they returned to Sing Sing state prison.

BLACKMAIL AND BANK ROBBERY

After her release from prison, Lyons expanded her criminal activities to include more profitable endeavors, such as blackmail (a form of extortion in which threats are used to gain payment) and bank robbery. Following circuses from one town to another, she and a partner in crime robbed small banks while the employees watched the circus parade pass by. She also robbed banks by posing as a wealthy woman who was considering opening an account. First she and her accomplice waited until one clerk was alone in the bank. Her partner then convinced the clerk to speak to Lyons, who waited outside in an elegant carriage. Once the clerk was outside, Lyons held a long conversation with him—while her accomplice robbed the empty bank.

Lyons also employed blackmail to bolster her bank accounts. In one instance, she accompanied a married man to a room in a Boston hotel. She hid his clothing and threatened to expose him if he didn't agree to her demands. The man wrote her a check for several thousand dollars.

As her wealth mounted, Lyons took it upon herself to make up for the education she had not received as a child. Once illiterate, she hired tutors to teach her to read and write. She read literature and studied art and music—and reportedly learned to speak four languages. Traveling often to Europe, she moved among the upper class and pulled off a number of successful heists—from robbing banks to smuggling stolen gems.

THE BANK OF SOPHIE

In the early 1890s, Lyons opened the New York Women's Banking and Investment Company with another con artist, Carrie Morse. Lyons later described Morse in her memoirs (book about a person's life), in a chapter titled "Women Criminals of Extraordinary Ability with Whom I Was in Partnership." Morse had, according to Lyons, "well-bred cordiality which was such an important part of her stock in trade [an important part of her success as a con woman]." She further described her extraordinary partner: "In every detail, her well kept hands, her gentle voice, her superb complexion, and the dainty way she had of wearing her mass of chestnut hair—she was the personification [embodiment] of luxury and refinement." Lyons, meanwhile, posed as the bank's elegant president, Mrs. Celia Rigsby. Together they preyed on wealthy women—as well as poor elderly widows. Before the "bank" closed, it had collected at least $50,000 from unsuspecting victims. But Lyons did not profit from the scam. A veteran swindler, Morse double-crossed her partner and ran off with the money.

The queen of crime

By the 1880s, Lyons had such a famous criminal reputation that the chief of the New York Police Department, William S. Devery, held a special press conference to denounce the "Queen of Crime." He told newspaper reporters:

Sophie Lyons is one of the cleverest criminals that the country has ever produced. She has carried her operations into nearly every quarter of the civilized globe and is known to the police of every European capital. She has been arrested hundreds of times since she was first picked up by the police in 1859 at age twelve. And don't you believe that nonsense about her reforming. For her that's impossible.

RETIREMENT FROM A LIFE OF CRIME

Lyons soon retired from crime. Her long career as a criminal earned her the reputation as "the Queen of Crime"—and it had taken away her ability to operate anonymously (without being noticed). One police official commented, "Of late years, she has had little opportunity for plundering, for her face is so well known in all the large cities of America and Europe that she is constantly watched for, if she is not arrested on site." Adding to her difficulties was the fact that she was addicted to opium (a narcotic drug made from the poppy plant).

Claiming to be a reformed criminal, Lyons became a society columnist for the *New York World* newspaper. She also wrote an autobiography, titled *Why Crime Does Not Pay*. Published in

1913, it provided numerous accounts of crimes that paid—and paid well. Nonetheless, Lyons urged other criminals to give up their crooked occupations. She hoped that fellow swindler **Ellen Peck** (see entry) would read her book, and that the experience would help Peck to mend her criminal ways.

But not all of her subjects wanted to be reformed. On May 8, 1924, she let three men into her home—supposedly in the hope of reforming them. They asked her for the money and valuables that were reportedly hidden around her house. She refused. Her neighbors found her on the floor, in a coma. Her skull had been crushed. Taken to Grace Hospital in Detroit, Michigan, Lyons died later that evening of a massive brain hemorrhage. She was seventy-six years old.

Sources for Further Reading

Byrnes, Thomas. *1886 Professional Criminals of America.* Broomall, PA: Chelsea House, 1969, pp. 205–206.

De Grave, Kathleen. *Swindler, Spy, Rebel.* Columbia: University of Missouri Press, 1995, pp. 57–73, 144–157.

Nash, Jay Robert. *Look for the Woman: A Narrative Encyclopedia of Female Poisoners, Kidnappers, Thieves, Extortionists, Terrorists, Swindlers, and Spies from Elizabethan Times to Present.* New York: M. Evans, 1981, pp. 321–322.

Ellen Peck
(Nellie Crosby)

Born: 1829
Died: 1915

Referred to as the "Queen of Confidence Women," Ellen Peck came up with ingenious (creative) plans to swindle wealthy victims—even as an old woman.

WORTHLESS INFORMATION

Born Nellie Crosby in Woodville, New Hampshire, in 1829, Peck eventually settled in New York City. She was an ordinary swindler until 1878, when she gained notoriety (attention) for cheating B. T. Babbitt, a wealthy soap manufacturer, out of $19,000. Babbitt had recently been robbed of more than $500,000 and was eager to recover his lost money. Posing as a female detective, Peck promised to produce valuable information in the robbery. But she needed a cash advance. The elderly millionaire advanced her the money—and soon discovered that the information she provided was worthless. Although Babbitt attempted to bring Peck to trial, she continued to swindle (cheat people out of money) unsuspecting victims—including other swindlers.

Samuel Pingee, a man who dealt with patented (certified) drugs, paid her for inside information on stock investments. Claiming that she received stock tips from a friend in the office of Jay Gould, a wealthy investor, Peck collected $2,700 from

Pingee. Again, the information Peck provided was worthless. John D. Grady, a shady diamond dealer, was also among Peck's victims. A veteran swindler, Grady lent the confidence woman (female con artist or swindler) a large sum of cash in exchange for the receipt to a safe deposit vault that supposedly contained valuable diamonds. The vault was empty.

STOLEN JEWELRY

Four years after the Babbitt affair, detectives caught up with Peck. Although she was formally charged with the crime, her trial received several postponements. When the date of her trial approached, she claimed—repeatedly—to be ill. When that ploy no longer worked, she pretended to be insane and was sent to an asylum (a type of hospital that treats the mentally ill) in Pennsylvania. On July 18, 1879, she was tried in the Kings County Court of Sessions on another charge—obtaining several thousand dollars' worth of jewelry under false pretenses. But she managed again to avoid a conviction.

NEW SCAM

Peck soon engaged in other scams in which she passed herself off as Mrs. Eliza Knight, a woman who held a large bank account at a New York bank. First she introduced herself as Mrs. Knight to John H. Johnson, a Manhattan jeweler. She selected $150 in jewelry, for which she gave Johnson $25. Using the bank where Knight had an account as a reference, she promised to pay the remaining $125 at a later date. Convinced that her credit was worthy, Johnson allowed Peck to leave with the jewelry. But he soon found out that the woman who visited him was not the Mrs. Knight who enjoyed good credit at the bank.

Peck borrowed Mrs. Knight's identity again on March 4, 1884, when she introduced herself to a diamond dealer named John Bough. Claiming to be a businesswoman who dealt in precious stones, she selected a diamond ring valued at $75. She said the ring was for a woman friend. Peck returned the next day to pay Bough the money she owed. Hoping that she might bring him additional business, he offered to pay her a commission (fee). Peck refused, saying that the purchase was insignificant. But she promised, however, to return soon to place a more important order.

The following month Peck informed Bough that she was going to meet with a wealthy woman from Brooklyn. Claiming that she could sell the woman some jewelry, she chose $400 worth of diamond earrings and rings. Bough waited several days for Peck to return with either a payment or the jewelry, but she never appeared.

"The psychology of women"

In 1895, *Popular Science Monthly* printed an article by G. T. W. Patrick, a prominent psychiatrist. Titled "The Psychology of Women," the article reflected the common belief at that time, that women were, by nature, deceptive. "[A woman's] greatest moral defect is her untruthfulness," Patrick wrote. "Deception and ruse [misleading actions] in woman, far more than in man, have become a habit of thought and speech."

The jeweler reported the incident to the police, who discovered that the missing diamonds had been left at a pawnshop called Simpson's. Sometime after the jewelry had been exchanged for $130, Peck entered the shop with a claim ticket. She told the shopkeeper the jewels had been stolen from her, and that she had received the claim ticket in the mail. When the shop owner refused to turn over the jewelry, Peck brought the matter to court. The suit was tried on September 12, 1884. But the result was not what she had hoped: the judge postponed making a decision in the case and Bough, meanwhile, had identified the jewelry as his missing property.

Borrowed money

Soon Peck swindled another victim, a woman named Ann McConnell. Posing as a woman named Mrs. Crosby, Peck claimed that she needed money to help her son start a business. She also claimed that she had a substantial income, but would not have access to her next payment until May and that she had a house on Putnam Avenue in Brooklyn that was filled with furniture that could be used as collateral (property that is pledged to protect the lender). Impressed by Peck's elegant manner, McConnell lent her $250. "Mrs. Crosby" agreed to pay back the loan—plus a $75 interest fee—in thirty days.

A little over two weeks later, McConnell read about a woman who had been arrested for swindling a jeweler. The woman lived on Putnam Avenue. She wondered if it could be the "Mrs. Crosby" who had borrowed money from her. When McConnell left the Tombs Police Court, where Peck was being held, there was no doubt. Peck was the woman who had introduced herself as Mrs. Crosby.

McConnell was not surprised when, at the end of thirty days, Peck had not repaid the loan. On December 6, 1884, the con woman was again led into police custody. The charge was larceny (theft). Her lawyer, Henry A. Meyenborg, argued that his client's failure to pay the debt and interest was not equal to the charge of larceny. She was set free.

A JAILBIRD AND A CON

Finally, on October 6, 1885, Peck received her first conviction. Charged with forging (faking) a document in order to obtain $3,000 from the Mutual Life Insurance Company of New York City, she was sentenced to four and a half years in prison. When she heard the sentence, Peck reportedly started to faint and then wept uncontrollably. At the age of fifty-six, she headed for the penitentiary on Blackwell's Island in New York.

Prison did not convince Peck to abandon the life of a con woman. In 1894 she played the role of an admiral's wife. Posing as the spouse of a Danish Navy officer, Admiral Johann Carl Hansen, she collected more than $50,000 in loans from various banks. Shortly thereafter she managed to swindle $10,000 from an elderly Brooklyn physician named Dr. Christopher Lott. She was arrested one last time in 1913 for cheating a Latin-American businessman who had given her the title to several coffee plantations. Peck died two years later, at the age of eighty-six.

Large savings account

Peck reportedly had more than $1 million stashed in numerous bank accounts when she died at the ripe old age of eighty-six.

Sources for Further Reading

Byrnes, Thomas. *1886 Professional Criminals of America.* Broomall, PA: Chelsea House, 1969, pp. 316–321.

De Grave, Kathleen. *Swindler, Spy, Rebel.* Columbia: University of Missouri Press, 1995, pp. 57–73, 144–157.

Nash, Jay Robert. *Look for the Woman: A Narrative Encyclopedia of Female Poisoners, Kidnappers, Thieves, Extortionists, Terrorists, Swindlers, and Spies from Elizabethan Times to Present.* New York: M. Evans, 1981, pp. 321–322.

Charles Ponzi

Born: 1883
Died: 1949

Sometimes referred to as the "Boston Swindler," Charles Ponzi set in motion one of the largest financial hoaxes of the twentieth century. Although he was widely regarded as a financial genius, he was nothing more than an inept (foolish) risk taker who enjoyed a brief bout of good luck.

POOR BEGINNINGS

Born in Italy in 1883, Ponzi emigrated (moved) to the United States when he was about twenty years old. Having entered his adoptive country with only $2.50, he became a waiter, but was soon fired. Still very poor, he took a train to Canada, where he was arrested for forging (faking) a check. Ponzi was sentenced to a brief term in a Montreal prison, after which he returned to the United States. In Atlanta, Georgia, he came up with a scheme to help Italians enter the country illegally—without following proper immigration procedures. Ponzi soon found himself in prison again—this time for smuggling aliens (transporting people illegally) into the United States.

Ponzi headed north to Boston, Massachusetts, in 1914. After marrying a woman named Rose, he assumed control of his father-in-law's grocery business. When that failed, he took a job as a translator for an import-export firm, which paid only $16 per week. While working at the firm, Ponzi came across something that gave him an idea for a scheme to earn money quickly.

Ponzi discovered that International Postal Union reply coupons could be purchased in Europe at a low rate, because the economies of European countries were depressed. The coupons could then be redeemed in the United States—which was not suffering from an economic depression at that time—for a much higher rate. Ponzi used these reply coupons as a foreign exchange system: buying inflated foreign currencies, swapping the money for international exchange coupons, and reconverting these coupons into dollars.

THE SECURITIES EXCHANGE COMPANY

Ponzi was convinced that he had found his calling. He quit his job to focus on the postal coupon business and borrowed money to purchase his first batch. His plan was slow to develop because various rules and regulations made it difficult to redeem the coupons. But eventually the scheme began to pay off—handsomely. For example, Ponzi was able to purchase coupons from his native country, Italy, at a cost of one cent each. He then had the coupons mailed to him in the United States, where he redeemed them for five cents each—for a profit of four cents per coupon.

Ponzi was not content to limit himself to a one-man operation. He convinced other investors to take part, promising them an astonishing 50 percent profit within three months. Ponzi's offer was too good to refuse. Investors flocked to his seedy (rundown) office at 27 School Street in Boston's financial district. So much money passed through the Securities Exchange Company that his employees stashed it in trash cans, drawers, and closets. And Ponzi made good on his promise. He paid old investors with cash supplied by new investors, doubling their money within six months. Hailed as the "Wizard of Finance," Ponzi collected *$15 million* from forty thousand investors over an eight-month period that began in December 1919. His best single-day take amounted to more than $2 million.

The greatest Italian of them all

When Charles "Get Rich Quick" Ponzi was called to a hearing to investigate his financial operations, he was tremendously popular among the people of Boston—many of whom he had helped to collect a small fortune. As he entered the city's State House—wearing a straw hat, walking stick, and boutonniere (a lapel flower)—he was cheered by enthusiastic crowds. Some onlookers reportedly praised him as "the greatest Italian of them all." Ponzi is said to have responded, "No, [Christopher] Columbus and [Guglielmo] Marconi were greater. Columbus discovered America, Marconi discovered the wireless." To this, a voice in the crowd added, "But you discovered money!"

Crowds gather outside
Charles Ponzi's Boston
office, 1920.

Ponzi was so successful that he opened branch offices throughout New England, New Jersey, and New York. He bought an extravagant mansion, a chauffeur-driven limousine, hundreds of expensive suits and ties, gold-handled walking canes, and diamond stickpins. Having made thousands of other investors wealthy, he enjoyed the respect and affection of the community—for a while.

BORROWING FROM PETER TO PAY PAUL

Ponzi's plan worked without a hitch—as long as there was a ready flow of incoming cash. But after about six months of money-trading, the local newspapers began to look into his operations. At first, Ponzi stalled the investigations by striking back with large lawsuits. Before long, the *Boston Post* newspaper uncovered Ponzi's criminal record, which included convictions for forgery and smuggling aliens.

The news startled Ponzi's investors. The company's steady flow of new clients came to an abrupt end—and former investors demanded their money back. Without incoming cash to pay out interest on old investments, Ponzi's scheme fell to pieces. He ordered his clerks to pay off his clients, but there was not enough money to cover his debts. The Securities Exchange Company paid out $15 million—leaving about $5 million in unpaid debts.

State investigators were appalled at the state of Ponzi's bookkeeping. Instead of careful records of cash receipts and payments, they found pages of random entries—some of which were missing dates, names, or amounts. Soon federal agents arrested Ponzi. Because he had written letters to clients asking them to reinvest, he was charged with using the U.S. mails to commit fraud, or deliberate deception. He served four years in a Plymouth, Massachusetts, prison for mail fraud. Released in 1925, Ponzi was arrested again for his swindle, but this time he was charged with theft. Sentenced to a nine-year term, he posted bail and fled to Florida.

A FLORIDA LAND SCAM

Ponzi arrived in Florida at a time when the southern state was in the midst of booming real estate speculation and land sales. He set up a land swindle, promising a 200-percent profit to his clients—and was soon arrested and convicted. After serving one year in a Florida prison he was released. He was then forced to return to Massachusetts to serve out his original nine-year sentence for theft. Ponzi was paroled (granted early release) in 1934—and deported to Naples, Italy, as an undesirable alien.

What Ponzi did next is not entirely clear. He seems to have secured a position in the government of Italian dictator Benito Mussolini (1883–1945). Within a few years he left Italy for South America. Sources vary on the reasons for his departure.

He died penniless

Shortly before Ponzi died in Rio de Janeiro in 1949, the press carried one of the former swindler's final public statements. He said, "I guess the only news about me that most people want to hear is my death." Once a millionaire, Ponzi died penniless in the charity ward of a Brazilian hospital.

According to one version, he traveled to Rio de Janeiro, Brazil, to manage Italy's LATI Airlines. According to another story, Ponzi was forced to flee from his native country because he had been discovered skimming money from the government's treasury. In any case, Ponzi settled in Rio de Janeiro. Partially blind and paralyzed, he eventually landed in the charity ward of a Brazilian hospital, where he died in January 1949, at the age of sixty-six. Ponzi's funeral reportedly took his last $75.

Sources for Further Reading

"Charles Ponzi." *Newsweek Obituaries* (January 31, 1949), p. 55.

Nash, Jay Robert. *Bloodletters and Badmen.* New York: M. Evans, 1973, pp. 252, 382–387.

"One of the Slickest of Them All." *Newsweek* (April 1, 1957), pp. 93–94.

Sifakis, Carl. *The Encyclopedia of American Crime.* New York: Facts on File, 1982, pp. 582–583.

"Take My Money!" *Time* (January 31, 1949), p. 21.

Joseph Weil

Born: 1875 or 1877

Died: February 26, 1976
AKA: Dr. Tourneur St. Harriot,
Walter H. Weed, James R. Wilson,
The Yellow Kid

Considered to be one of the greatest con men of the twentieth century, Joseph Weil posed as a number of characters to pull off elaborate scams. Looking back on his career Weil once commented: "Men like myself could not have existed without the victims' covetous [desirous], criminal greed."

THE YELLOW KID

Although Weil claimed to have been born in Chicago in 1875, some records indicate that the year of his birth was actually 1877. He was raised in Chicago and began to associate with crooks at an early age. As a teenager, Weil was fond of reading a popular comic strip, "Hogan's Alley and the Yellow Kid," which appeared in the *New York Journal.* He soon picked up a nickname—the Yellow Kid—that would follow him throughout his life.

Weil was married at an early age. Although his wife wanted him to lead an honest life, he was involved in numerous scams over a period of about forty years. A well-dressed, impressive looking man, he wore a carefully groomed beard and either a monocle (an eyeglass for one eye) or pince-nez (eyeglasses that are clipped to the bridge of the nose). Sometimes he dressed in a beaver hat and cape and yellow gloves. Weil's dignified and affluent (wealthy) appearance helped him to convince his victims that he was a banker, millionaire, or whatever role his scam required him to play.

Weil often worked with other con men who helped him pull off elaborate scams. In 1908, he first hooked up with Fred "the Deacon" Buckminster—a man who would become a longtime criminal associate. The two reportedly met when Buckminster, who was a Chicago policeman, arrested Weil, who had duped (tricked) clients into paying him to paint buildings with a phony "waterproofing" substance. But before Weil arrived at the precinct house, he convinced the policeman that he had earned thousands of dollars through confidence scams (scams that rely on the victim's trust). Tempted by the prospect of easy money, Buckminster teamed with Weil in a number of schemes over the next twenty-five years.

MAN'S BEST FRIEND

Weil once appeared in a Chicago bar with a dog. He informed the bartender that he had an errand to run, and asked the man to watch his dog. He claimed the animal was a valuable, prize-winning pedigreed (pure-bred) hunting dog—and he had the papers to prove it.

Weil left the dog with the bar owner. Soon another man appeared. The man—who was actually working with Weil—admired the dog and offered to pay the bartender as much as $300. The bartender informed him that he could not sell the dog because it was not his. The man then offered him $50 as a deposit. He also left a phone number where the bartender was to call him in case the dog's owner was willing to sell his pet.

When Weil returned to the saloon, the bartender offered to buy the dog. At first Weil objected—to make sure that the man did not become suspicious. Eventually, he accepted $250 from the bartender, who planned to call the man who had offered him $300 for the dog. But the man's phone number was fake—as were the dog's awards and papers.

A FREE LAND FLIMFLAM

When he was still in his twenties, Weil teamed with a former riverboat gambler named Colonel (pronounced KER-nel)

Jim Porter. First, the pair purchased land in Michigan for $1 per acre. Then Weil introduced Porter as an eccentric (unconventional) millionaire who was giving away valuable land *for nothing*. Bartenders, waiters, prostitutes, and even policemen accepted free parcels of land from Weil's supposed millionaire friend. Once the victim accepted the land, Weil made a point of asking him or her to keep quiet about it—since there were not enough free lots to go around.

Weil and Porter also opened a phony sales office that displayed a lavish plan to turn the land into a large, expensive vacation area. Convinced that the free land would soon become even more valuable, Weil's victims followed his advice to record the land transaction at the Michigan county seat. Recording the land transfer would allow them to prove that they owned the lots when they were ready to sell the parcels to the supposed vacation area developers.

It was no coincidence that the county recorder was Porter's cousin. The usual recording fee was just $2. But the recorder raised the price to $30—of which $15 went to Weil and Porter. The pair reportedly earned well over $15,000 in recorder's fees in what became known as the "Great Michigan Free Land Swindle."

A COLOSSAL BANK SCAM

Many of Weil's scams involved numbers of other participants and elaborate props. In one of his most complicated schemes, Weil learned that the Merchants National Bank in Muncie, Indiana, was vacating its original building to move to another location. After arranging to rent the original building—which still contained the tellers' cages—he stocked it with deposit and withdrawal slips that had been stolen from other banks as well as salt sacks for money bags. His associates posed as bank tellers, security guards, and regular customers.

Weil, in the meantime, had been trying to convince a millionaire to invest $50,000 in a phony land deal. To close the deal, he told the millionaire that the president of the Muncie bank was in favor of the transaction. The man was not from Muncie and was therefore unaware that the bank had moved—and that the

Honor among thieves

In 1956, Weil was called to testify before a Senate subcommittee, led by Senator Estes Kefauver, that was investigating juvenile delinquency (crimes committed by young people). Eighty-one years old and retired from swindling, Weil was appalled at the lack of honor among swindlers. He claimed that in his day, a swindler never left his victim penniless. "Our victims were mostly big industrialists and bankers," he testified. "The old-time confidence men had a saying: 'Never send them to the river [leave them with nothing].' We never picked on poor people or cleaned them out completely. Taking the life savings from poor old women is just the same as putting a revolver to her head and pressing the trigger!"

Weil also told the committee that he regretted his crimes. "I see how despicable [hateful] were the things I did," he said. "I found out a man is responsible not only for himself but for the other lives he wrecked."

supposed bank president was a con artist and friend of Weil's. When the millionaire visited the bank, he was impressed by its apparent success. The bank's "president" had no trouble convincing him that the land deal was a worthwhile investment. Weil collected some $50,000 from his victim and then closed the "bank."

A MINING MILLIONAIRE

Weil often made his scams appear more believable by using forged (faked) documents. In order to convince victims that he was a mining millionaire, he devised an elaborate ruse (deception) with an associate who was a printer. Weil gave the printer a copy of *McClure's,* a financial magazine. The issue included a story about Pope Yateman, a man who had earned millions from an abandoned gold mine he had purchased in Chile, a country in South America. The printer substituted Weil's photograph for that of Yateman—and then reprinted the page and rebound the magazine.

Weil traveled to various cities in the Midwest with the doctored (altered) magazine issue. First he visited the town library, where he replaced the library's copy with his phony reprint. Next he posed as a mining millionaire who was passing through town. He targeted wealthy victims and informed them that he had made a fortune by investing in an abandoned gold mine. And he suggested that they read about it in the local library. Impressed by the article in *McClure's,* a number of people gave Weil money to invest for them. Once he had collected sufficient funds, Weil left town—but not until after he replaced the reprinted magazine with the authentic library copy so that no one could identify him after the scam was discovered.

AN HONEST CITIZEN

Weil's victims rarely reported him to the authorities. Over the course of forty years of operations, he served only three prison terms, which amounted to less than six years' imprisonment. He was last convicted in 1940, when he was sentenced to three years for a mail-fraud (using the mail service as a means to deliberately deceive) charge involving phony oil leases. Released after only twenty-seven months, he settled in Chicago, where he abandoned swindling to live a law-abiding life.

In 1948, Weil wrote his memoirs—*The Autobiography of Yellow Kid Weil*—with the help of a Chicago journalist named W. T. Brannon. In his autobiography he claimed that he had earned about $8 million in four decades of international operations. (Some authorities believe he exaggerated his earnings, estimating that he collected only $3 to $5 million—still, a large amount of money.) At the time of his death, Weil had no money left. The cost of operating his scams had been enormous, and his attempts to invest in legitimate businesses had failed. Weil entered the Chicago Lake Front Convalescent Center on welfare (public relief) when he was in his nineties. He often said that he wanted to live to be one hundred years old. Weil died on February 26, 1976. Newspapers listed his age as one hundred—although records suggest that he was only ninety-nine.

Easy targets

Weil once boasted that "I never found a man I couldn't take." He reportedly swindled a police detective out of $30,000 for phony stock—as the detective escorted him to Joliet Prison in Illinois on a swindling charge.

Sources for Further Reading

"Joseph Weil." *The New York Times Obituaries* (February 27, 1976), p. 34.

"Joseph Weil." *Newsweek Obituaries* (March 8, 1976), p. 37.

"Joseph Weil." *Time Obituaries* (March 8, 1976), p. 81.

Nash, Jay Robert. *Bloodletters and Badmen.* New York: M. Evans, 1973, pp. 598–601.

"One of the Slickest of Them All." *Newsweek* (April 1, 1957), pp. 93–94.

Sifakis, Carl, *The Encyclopedia of American Crime.* New York: Facts on File, 1982, pp. 751–752.

"The Yellow Kid Returns." *Newsweek* (December 24, 1956), pp. 20–21.

Take a look at this!
Dirty Rotten Scoundrels (1988) features Steve Martin and Michael Caine as con men who attempt to rip off a suddenly rich woman--and each other.

Terrorists

Terrorists employ violence to intimidate, to protest, to incite revolution. Their motives are many but their methods invariably rely on the use of deadly force. They commit appalling acts of violence against innocent victims for which they are regarded by some as enemies of mankind.

Included in this section are profiles of four terrorists: JoAnne Chesimard, an African American revolutionary accused of murdering a New Jersey state trooper; Gordon Kahl, a tax protester who died in an explosive battle with FBI agents; Timothy McVeigh, who was convicted of what is considered to be the worst act of terrorism on American soil; and Diana Oughton, who perished when the bomb factory belonging to a terrorist group known as the Weathermen exploded.

You'll read about Timothy McVeigh's childhood, his wartime experiences, and his disturbing obsession with weapons. You'll learn about the right-wing belief system that led Gordon Kahl to shoot at agents who served him papers for tax evasion. And you'll find out much about the social climate of the 1970s—an era marked by peaceful civil rights demonstrations, student protests, and antiwar activities, as well as violent terrorist acts committed by radical organizations.

JoAnne Chesimard
(Assata Shakur)

Born: July 16, 1947
AKA: Joan Davis, Justine Henderson

To the FBI, JoAnne Chesimard is an armed robber, a cop-killer, and a dangerous escaped criminal. To her supporters, she is a woman of action who has never received fair treatment from the law. Whatever she may be to others, Chesimard is—by her own description—a black revolutionary.

FROM NEW YORK TO NORTH CAROLINA

Chesimard was born JoAnne Deborah Byron in New York City on July 16, 1947. Until she was three, she lived with her parents, her aunt, and her grandparents in a house in Flushing, New York. Her father was an accountant for the federal government and her mother taught elementary school. When her parents divorced, Chesimard accompanied her grandparents, Frank and Lulu Hill, to Wilmington, North Carolina.

In a place where African Americans were barred from public beaches, her grandparents owned property and became small business owners. They ran a beach-front restaurant with lockers and changing rooms that provided a vacationing spot for many people who had never seen the ocean. Chesimard helped out at the restaurant and spent much of her time playing on the beach and reading the stacks of books her grandfather had brought her from the "colored" library.

Mistreatment in jail

In her autobiography, Chesimard denies that she shot at anyone during the shootout on the New Jersey turnpike. She also claims that the incident gave her a reputation as a militant (combative) cop-killer—a reputation that brought her mistreatment and neglect throughout her imprisonment. She writes of being harassed and even tortured by police in the hospital. And she tells of being moved from New York's Roosevelt Hospital to a county workhouse in Middlesex, New Jersey, where she was denied physical therapy for her injuries.

DIFFERENT FORMS OF RACISM

Because Chesimard's grandparents were afraid that the segregated (racially separated) North Carolina school system was providing their grandchild with an inferior education, they sent her back to New York to live with her mother and stepfather. The eight-year-old was shifted from one extreme to another. She left a segregated, all-African American community in the South for a middle-class, heavily Jewish, and nearly all-white area of Queens, New York.

There she encountered a new kind of racism. In third and fourth grades, Chesimard was the only African American child in her class. In the fifth grade she was one of only two. As one of a very small minority in her school, she ran into teachers and students who assumed she was inferior because of her color. She attended schools where African American children were sometimes automatically placed in slow classes because teachers and administrators assumed they were not as bright and capable as white students.

Like most African American children of the 1950s, she was never allowed to forget that she was different because she was black. "When I was growing up," she revealed in her autobiography, "being called 'Black,' period, was ground for fighting."

ASSATA SHAKUR

Chesimard dropped out of high school and began running away from home. She searched for odd jobs and tried to make it on her own, but life on the streets brought its own kind of education. She stayed briefly with a family of professional shoplifters, and found herself in more than one dangerous situation. When her aunt, a lawyer named Evelyn Williams, found her and took her home, the thirteen-year-old was working in a bar hustling drinks. Chesimard credited her aunt for expanding her education by introducing her to culture, museums, and theater, and for seeing to it that she got her Graduate Equivalent

Degree (GED) after she quit high school at the age of sixteen.

In the late 1960s, Chesimard entered Manhattan Community College. She planned to major in business administration, but was immediately drawn to the school's expanding black studies program and the activities of the student body. At a time when the African American struggle and consciousness were on the upswing, she began to read about black history, culture, politics, and ideology (belief systems). She attended civil rights meetings and took part in passionate discussions. She joined a black students' group called the "Society of the Golden Drums," where she met her husband, Louis Chesimard. She even changed her hair and dress to reflect her African roots. She also took on a Muslim name, Assata Shakur. "It was like being born again," she wrote. "It was then that I decided that the most important thing in my life was for me to struggle for the liberation of black people."

THE BLACK LIBERATION ARMY

In 1970, Chesimard joined the Black Panther Party (BPP) and was assigned to provide assistance to the African American community through medical care and the breakfast program. But like many other members, she soon became disappointed with the BPP. She left the party after coming to the conclusion that its lack of a unifying philosophy made the party weak and ineffective.

Chesimard turned to a more radical (revolutionary) organization—the Black Liberation Army (BLA). Members of the informally organized BLA believed that change would come about through revolution. From 1971 to 1973, the BLA was held responsible for a series of sniper shootings and bank robberies in New York, New Jersey, Missouri, and Michigan. JoAnne Chesimard, as the news media continued to call her, was considered to be the guiding force behind the BLA.

In *Assata: An Autobiography,* Chesimard recalls how her grandparents tried to instill in her a sense of personal dignity and self-esteem. "I was to be polite and respectful to adults," she wrote, "but when it came to dealing with white people in the segregated South, my grandmother would tell me menacingly, 'Don't you respect nobody that don't respect you, you hear me?'"

LEGAL TROUBLES

Chesimard was personally charged with six different crimes, including bank robbery and the attempted murder of police officers. In 1974, she and Fred Hilton, another reputed member of the BLA, were tried for robbing a bank in the Bronx, New York, in September of 1972. (They had already been tried once for the robbery. The trial resulted in a hung jury—a jury that cannot agree on a verdict—with eleven of the twelve jurors in favor of a guilty verdict.) During the second trial, both Chesimard and Hilton were forced to leave the courtroom because they shouted insults at the judge. They also claimed to reject the U.S. legal system. Chesimard acted as her own lawyer through part of the trial, and helped to show that some of the testimony against her was inconsistent. Both Chesimard and Hilton were acquitted (found not guilty).

But Chesimard remained in jail on charges of murder. On May 2, 1973, the car that she and her two companions were traveling in was stopped by the police on the New Jersey turnpike. Gunfire was exchanged. A New Jersey state trooper and a former Black Panther information minister lay dead. Chesimard was wounded in both arms and a shoulder. The second man fled. The following day the *New York Times* reported that, at the time of her arrest, Chesimard was wanted by the Federal Bureau of Investigation (FBI) for armed bank robbery and by the New York police in connection with the 1972 slaying of two policemen, as well as for a hand-grenade attack on a police car.

During the beginning of the state trooper murder trial, Chesimard had discovered that she was pregnant. The father was Fred Hilton, her co-defendant in the bank robbery trial. The news of her pregnancy made headlines, but it did not improve her living conditions. She was taken from the prison on Rikers Island to the Middlesex County jail, where she spent more than twenty months in solitary confinement. (A prisoner in solitary confinement is not allowed contact with other inmates.) On September 11, 1974, she gave birth to her daughter, Kakuya Amala Olugbala Shakur, at a local hospital. A few days later, Chesimard was returned to Rikers Island.

A mistrial was declared because of Chesimard's pregnancy. But three years later a new murder trial was held. On March 25, 1977, Chesimard was convicted of the murder of the New Jersey state trooper. Because she was found guilty of murdering a law enforcement official, the sentence was severe. Chesimard was sentenced to life in prison—plus twenty-six to thirty-three years, to be served one after the other. (Sometimes life sentences are shortened, and the convict is paroled, or released before serving out the full sentence. In some cases, time is added to a life sentence to make sure that the convict spends a life term in prison.)

JAIL BREAK

In 1978, Chesimard was transferred to a maximum security prison for women in West Virginia. But because the facility was being closed down and other prisons considered her too great a security risk, she was shipped back to the New Jersey Corrections Institute for Women. Then, on November 2, 1979, three visitors seized two prison guards at gunpoint and took control of a prison van. Chesimard escaped. The following day she was named to the FBI's most wanted list.

With the help of her supporters, Chesimard managed to avoid capture for five years. Authorities suspected that the Weathermen (a violent and extreme group of radicals) might have helped her hide from police. In 1984, Chesimard was granted political asylum (political protection) in Cuba. She slipped out of the United States—and beyond the jurisdiction (authority) of U.S. law. Because the FBI kept her friends and family under close surveillance, Chesimard could not risk contacting them until she was out of the country. But once in Cuba, she was visited several times by her mother and her Aunt Evelyn. And in 1987, her daughter, Kakuya, by then a pre-teen, went to live with her.

At the time, Chesimard was reportedly pursuing a master's degree and living in a government-paid apartment in Havana, Cuba. Also in 1987, Chesimard published her autobiography. On

The building in Pittsburgh, Pennsylvania, where FBI agents found evidence that JoAnne Chesimard had been using a second-floor apartment as a hideout.

March 29, 1998, New Jersey governor Christie Whitman announced that she would be appealing to Cuba for Chesimard's return.

Sources for Further Reading

Bacon, John. "Governor to appeal for convict's return." *USA Today* (March 31, 1998), p. 3A.

"Extremists Acquitted." *Time* (January 7, 1974), p. 24.

Shakur, Assata. *Assata: An Autobiography.* Chicago: Lawrence Hill Books, 1987.

"Then and Now, Revisiting the Radicals." *Newsweek* (September 27, 1993), p. 60.

"Three Still At Large." *Newsweek* (November 2, 1981), p. 33.

Gordon Kahl

Born: 1920
Died: June 4, 1983

A member of a right-wing fringe group, militant tax protestor Gordon W. Kahl vowed he would never be taken alive—and he was right.

A MAN WHO WOULD NOT PAY TAXES

Kahl, a retired North Dakota farmer, joined an extremely conservative survivalist group—an organization of militant individuals who do not recognize the government's authority. The group was known as the Posse Comitatus (Latin for "power of the county"). As a member of the organization, he was opposed to income taxes and most forms of government authority above the county level. To protest government taxation, Kahl refused to report his income to the federal government. In 1977, he was convicted of failing to file federal income tax returns, for which he was placed on probation. Like the other members of the Posse Comitatus, Kahl insisted on his right to carry firearms.

On February 13, 1983, federal marshals approached Kahl in Medina, North Dakota, to serve him with a warrant for violating his parole. (A prisoner who is placed on parole is expected to meet certain conditions.) A shootout followed—in which two marshals were killed. On May 11, Kahl, his twenty-three- year-old son Yorivon, and a man named Scott Faul were formally charged with the murders. Within three weeks, on May 28, Yorivon and Faul were convicted of two counts of second- degree murder. But Kahl, who had avoided capture, remained at large.

MANHUNT

The nationwide hunt for Gordon Kahl began in February 1983 and ended almost four months later, when Federal Bureau of Investigation (FBI) agents received a tip that someone answering to the fugitive's description was sighted near Smithville, Arkansas—a hilly area one hundred and twenty-five miles northeast of Little Rock. The informant recognized the man from a wanted poster. (It was not difficult to recognize a stranger in the area: Smithville at that time had only one hundred and thirteen residents.) The man who looked like Kahl was riding in a car that belonged to Leonard and Norma Ginter—a couple who were reportedly sided with tax protesters.

Officials knew that Kahl had spent the previous year living in Arkansas under a false name. In late May they set out to gather evidence that Kahl was residing with the Ginters in their bunker-like house four miles outside of Smithville—a hilly area populated by more than twenty tax protesters. Once they had adequate evidence to suggest that the Ginters were harboring the fugitive, officials obtained a search warrant. On June 2, federal officials staked out the Ginter home, which stood at the end of a mile-long dirt road. Constructed of concrete, the house was built partly underground. Ginter was known to collect large quantities of explosives, weapons, and ammunition.

After a two-day stakeout, federal marshals organized a raid on the Ginter house. At about 3 P.M. on June 4, heavily armed agents formed a large circle around the bunker—out of sight of its occupants. Backing them up were sheriff's deputies and state troopers. As an extra precaution, a fire truck and ambulance stood by as well.

Almost three hours later agents stopped Leonard Ginter as he drove away from his house—with a loaded and cocked gun in his lap. In the back seat was a loaded rifle with a telescopic sight—a weapon that allows the shooter to fire accurately from

a great distance. Before he was taken into custody, Ginter told officials that his wife was alone in the house.

SHOOTOUT NEAR SMITHVILLE

The Ginter house had only one door. After Ginter was stopped, Sheriff Gene Matthews led a state police investigator and two Federal agents through the door. As soon as they entered the house, Norma Ginter ran outside. And Kahl, who had been hiding behind a refrigerator, fired a high-powered rifle—striking the thirty-eight-year-old sheriff on his left side, between the flaps of his bullet-proof vest. Severely wounded, Matthews fired at Kahl as he crawled outside. The three other officers fired on Kahl as they left the house.

Once Matthews had been dragged away from the house, officers let loose a hail of automatic gunfire. They also fired smoke bombs through the windows of the home, hoping to force the fugitive outdoors. But the tactic backfired. One of the tear-gas canisters fell down an air vent and caught on fire, setting off an explosion of thousands of rounds of ammunition that had been stockpiled in the Ginter home. Inside the bunker, Kahl was trapped in a fireworks of exploding dynamite and ammunitions that went on for nearly two hours. The final ammunition explosion took place at 8:10 P.M.

The Ginter home continued to burn after the explosions ceased. Attempting to put out the blaze, fire fighters emptied the fire truck of its water supply. When officers entered the house at about 10 P.M., flames still smoldered in the ruins. Wearing face masks to avoid being overcome by the smoke, they found Kahl's body lying face down. An automatic weapon lay near his corpse. Around the same time that Kahl's body was being taken out of the fire-gutted house, Sheriff Matthews died of his wounds.

Sources for Further Reading

Corcoran, James. *Bitter Harvest: Gordon Kahl and the Posse Comitatus.* New York: Viking, 1990.

"Shootout In a Sleepy Hamlet." *Time* (June 13, 1983), p. 16.

Rawls, Wendell Jr. "Man Dead in Gunfight Identified as Dakota Fugitive." *The New York Times* (June 5, 1983), p. 18.

Timothy McVeigh

Born: April 23, 1968

When a bomb exploded in Oklahoma City, Oklahoma, in 1995, it killed and injured hundreds of innocent victims. The nation was stunned to discover that the attack had not been committed by international terrorists, but by an American whose background was hardly cause for concern.

A SCRAWNY KID FOND OF GUNS

Students in McVeigh's high school referred to their classmate as the school's "most talkative" student. They were kidding. Raised in a suburb of Buffalo, New York, McVeigh was a quiet boy who kept to himself. His classmates picked on him, calling him "Chicken McVeigh" and "The Wimp."

By the time he graduated from high school in Pendleton, New York, McVeigh had become obsessed with guns. He lifted weights in order to add muscle to his scrawny physique. And he became increasingly fascinated with extremist organizations (radical, right-wing groups that favor revolutionary changes in the government). An accomplished computer student, McVeigh earned a scholarship to a state college after taking an advanced placement course in programming. But he dropped out of college within a few months because it took time away from his real interests: guns and the extremist underworld. McVeigh read right-wing materials and conversed with others who shared his increasingly paranoid world-view—a world-view that saw the

315

federal government as evil and the citizens as victims who would soon be enslaved.

IN THE ARMY

McVeigh enlisted in the army in 1988, hoping to find his way into the Special Forces (an elite branch of the military). At Fort Riley in Kansas, he was a disciplined, model soldier. There he became increasingly interested in extremist publications—including a book called *The Turner Diaries,* which tells a bloody story of race war and right-wing revolution. When the Gulf War erupted, McVeigh served as a gunner on a assault vehicle in Kuwait. He earned a Bronze Star for his wartime service—which has been the subject of conflicting accounts. For example, McVeigh informed his mother that Iraqi soldiers surrendered to him with their arms in the air. But friends heard gorier tales of his Desert Storm experiences, which included blowing up an Iraqi soldier. Also, an army pal reported that McVeigh had shot an enemy soldier—even though the captured soldier held his arms in the air as a gesture of surrender.

After McVeigh returned from the Gulf War, he went to Fort Bragg, North Carolina, to participate in a course to qualify for Special Forces training. In April 1991, he dropped out of the difficult three-week course, and resigned from the army. He served briefly in the National Guard, but soon found other ways to feed his fascination with guns and other weapons.

THE NICHOLS BROTHERS

By 1993, McVeigh had drifted to the farming community of Decker, Michigan, where James and Terry Nichols lived. He had met Terry Nichols, a quiet, aloof man, in the army. The two men shared a hatred for the federal government. Terry Nichols claimed that he wanted to secede (to withdraw formally from an organization) from the United States and gave up his citizenship. He turned in his voter-registration card claiming that he was a "nonresident alien" (an outsider).

Terry's older brother, James—an organic farmer—also despised the government. To show his contempt, he defaced

The front of the Alfred
P. Murrah building was
turned to rubble when
the bomb went off,
killing 168 people.

(spoiled the appearance of) U.S. money and gave up his passport. When his ex-wife sued for child support, he told the court that he was no longer a citizen of "your Defacto . . . government." Regarded as strange by other members of his community, he used peroxide (a bleaching agent that contains oxygen) to bathe and amused himself by building homemade bombs. James and Terry Nichols belonged to an extremist group called the Patriots—an organization of gun-carrying anarchists who do not recognize any of the government's laws or authority.

During his stay in Decker, McVeigh became immersed in the Nichols brothers' anti-government philosophy. He attended Patriots meetings where members warned that bankers and politicians would soon take over the country and plant comput-

A timeline to death row

November 1994
$60,000 in guns and valuables are stolen from an Arkansas gun dealer.

December 1994
McVeigh and Michael Fortier visit each floor of the nine-story Murrah federal building in Oklahoma City.

January 1995
McVeigh and Fortier travel to Kansas, where they pile guns into a rented car. Fortier drives the car to Kingman, Arizona.

February 1995
McVeigh joins Fortier in Kingman. The two men reportedly sell the stash of guns.

April 14, 1995
McVeigh arrives in Junction City, Kansas. He sells his car and makes a phone call to reserve a Ryder rental truck for April 17.

April 18, 1995
McVeigh reportedly assembles an ammonium nitrate bomb with the help of Terry Nichols.

April 19, 1995
The Murrah building is destroyed by a bomb. McVeigh is stopped by a highway patrolman and arrested for a routine traffic violation.

April 21, 1995
Just as he is about to be released from the Perry jail on $500 bail, McVeigh is identified as "John Doe Number One."

April 1997
McVeigh's trial begins.

May 29, 1997
The prosecution and defense teams present closing arguments to sum up their cases.

May 30–June 2, 1997
The jury decides on a verdict.

June 2, 1997
A federal jury finds McVeigh guilty of eleven counts of murder and conspiracy. Later that month he is sentenced to death.

---

er chips in enslaved citizens. As his hatred for the government grew, he became increasingly paranoid.

A LETHAL EXPLOSION

On April 19, 1995, a bomb exploded in the Alfred P. Murrah Federal Building in Oklahoma City, Oklahoma. Within eight seconds, the building was utterly destroyed. Each of the nine floors collapsed on top of one another. Inside were government employees and small children who were playing in the building's day-care center.

Rescue workers attempted to save victims who had narrowly escaped death and were trapped in the rubble of the destroyed building. The broken remains of concrete, glass, and metal stood twenty-seven feet deep. After the dust had settled, one hundred and sixty-eight corpses were identified—nineteen of which were children.

At first, investigators suspected that the bombers were international terrorists—possibly Islamic fanatics who were known to use car bombs such as the one that had blown up the Murrah building. Immediately after the crash, federal agents began to sift through the debris for clues about the bombing.

A COUPLE OF JOHN DOES

Shortly after the explosion, the first significant clue appeared. Richard Nichols, a maintenance worker, was parked two blocks away from the Murrah building when the explosion occurred. Just as Nichols and his wife were about to get into their car, a large piece of metal landed on top of the vehicle. When investigators examined the metal scrap, they discovered that it was a piece of the axle of a truck. (An axle is a supporting shaft on which a wheel revolves.) But the axle had not come from just any truck. It had come from the vehicle that contained what investigators were calling the "OK Bomb." (OK is the abbreviation for Oklahoma.)

The truck axle contained a vehicle identification number (VIN). (Every car and truck has a VIN, which must be recorded with every new owner.) Using the truck's VIN, investigators traced the truck to a 1993 Ford that was registered to a Ryder rental agency in Miami, Florida. Further investigation placed the truck closer to the bombing. The Ryder agency had assigned the vehicle to a body shop in Junction City, Kansas—just two-hundred seventy miles from Oklahoma City.

Looking for a target

McVeigh and his friend Michael Fortier cased the Murrah building in December 1994. They stopped on each of the nine floors. There is little doubt that they saw the America's Kids day-care center on the second floor, where dozens of children were playing when the bomb exploded on April 19, 1995. Nineteen children died in the explosion.

It's possible that McVeigh did not intend to stop with the bombing of the Murrah building in Oklahoma City. Witnesses saw him and another man wandering around federal buildings in Phoenix, Arizona, and Omaha, Nebraska. It's possible the two men were casing the buildings to determine whether they were suitable targets for future bombings.

Pancho Villa rides again

Even as a high school student, McVeigh was obsessed with guns. After graduating he took a job as an armored car guard. Armed like a soldier, he rode in an armored car that took money from department stores to a nearby bank. His everyday work weaponry included three guns: one holstered in a black military belt, one tucked into a strap on his leg, and a third concealed in a handbag. A former co-worker recalled that the scrawny McVeigh once showed up "looking like **Pancho Villa**" (see entry). He had belts of ammunition strapped across his chest and he carried an arsenal of firearms that included two pistols, a sawed-off shotgun, and a rifle equipped with a scope. McVeigh's boss eventually told his gun-crazy employee that he would have to shed some of his weapons if he wanted to continue work as an armed guard.

The truck helped agents move closer to the bombing suspects. On April 17—two days before the bombing—two men had rented the truck that was used in the bombing at Elliott's Body Shop in Junction City. Investigators quickly traced the driver's license numbers the men had used to rent the truck. The licenses and other pieces of identification were fakes. But based on the descriptions of employees, FBI artists sketched a likeness of both men. In no time, the drawings of the bombing suspects were televised across the world. Investigators did not know the real names of the suspects, who became known as "John Doe Number One" and "John Doe Number Two." (John Doe is a name that is often assigned to someone whose true identity is unknown.)

A ROUTINE TRAFFIC STOP

Less than two hours after the explosion, state trooper Charlie Hanger pulled over a young man for a routine traffic violation on Interstate 35 in Perry, Oklahoma—about sixty minutes north of Oklahoma City. The driver of the 1977 yellow Mercury had no license tags. But he did have a gun—a nine-millimeter semiautomatic pistol was tucked under his jacket. It was loaded with Black Talon bullets, commonly known as "cop killers," because they can penetrate bulletproof vests worn by law enforcement officers. Hanger arrested the man on traffic and weapons charges.

Without realizing it, Hanger had arrested the prime suspect in the Oklahoma bombing case. At the time of his arrest, McVeigh was wearing a T-shirt that said, "The tree of liberty must be refreshed from time to time with the blood of patriots and tyrants." His car contained further clues about his state of

John Doe

In spite of one of the most intense manhunts in the history of the FBI, investigators never discovered the true identity of the man known as John Doe Number Two.

mind, such as sections of *The Turner Diaries* that describe the bombing of FBI headquarters and a piece of paper containing a quote from the eighteenth-century American Revolutionary leader Samuel Adams (1722–1803). It said, "When the Government fears the people, there is liberty. When the people fear the Government, there is tyranny [power that is exercised unjustly]." McVeigh had written something beneath the quote: "Maybe now, there will be liberty."

McVeigh was held at the small jail in Perry while the minor traffic and weapons charges were processed. After two days, he came within moments of being released. But before he was allowed to leave the jail, the results of a computer search arrived. McVeigh had been identified as one of the men who had rented the Ryder truck. Investigators believed that he was John Doe Number One.

A TON OF FERTILIZER

McVeigh was formally charged with the destruction of federal property. As investigators looked into his background and activities, they discovered a trail of evidence that linked him to the bombing. When they searched the home of Terry Nichols (who had moved to Kansas), they found a slip of pink paper in a drawer. It was a receipt for two thousand pounds of ammonium nitrate—a fertilizer that can be used as a key ingredient for bomb making. Although the receipt was made out to "Mike Havens," it provided a critical link to McVeigh: it contained his fingerprints.

The evidence against McVeigh was damning: neither he nor Nichols were farming at the time the fertilizer was purchased. With no crops, he had no real reason to purchase two thousand pounds of fertilizer. What's more, the bomb that destroyed the Murrah building contained a large quantity of ammonium nitrate. And the clothing McVeigh was wearing when he was arrested contained traces of a substance similar to the explosive.

The evidence against McVeigh mounted. Investigators also found his fingerprints on a rental contract for a storage unit where the ammonium nitrate was reportedly kept before the bomb was assembled. And the damp ground in front of the stor-

Recipe for disaster

Investigators determined that an ammonium nitrate bomb—sometimes called an "anfo"—destroyed the Murrah building in Oklahoma City. The Oklahoma bomber mixed 4,800 pounds of the fertilizer, ammonium nitrate, with fuel oil in twenty blue plastic drums. The bomb's destructive power was made even more deadly by the addition of metal containers of hydrogen or acetylene (a highly explosive gas).

age unit contained tire tracks that could have been made by a Ryder truck—such as the one McVeigh had rented in Kansas City.

Posing as job hunters

The fact that the Murrah building was so totally destroyed was no accident. The bomber—who was thoroughly familiar with the layout of the building—knew exactly how much explosive material to use and where to place it. Soon after McVeigh's arrest, federal investigators learned that witnesses had seen him casing the building (examining a building carefully in order to plan a crime) with another man.

Michael Fortier, an army buddy of McVeigh's, quit his job at the True Value Hardware store in Kingman, Arizona, on December 22, 1994. Later that month, he and McVeigh traveled to Oklahoma City, where they visited each of the nine floors of the Murrah building. They avoided attracting attention by posing as men looking for jobs at the offices of various federal agencies—such as the Small Business Administration and the Internal Revenue Service.

The case against McVeigh

After two years of pretrial proceedings—which produced seven thousand pounds of physical evidence and twenty-five thousand interviews—McVeigh's trial began in Denver, Colorado, in April 1997. (Terry Nichols was tried in a separate trial.) U.S. assistant attorney Joseph Hartzler, who led the prosecution team, promised to try the case in just six weeks. Many people thought Hartzler would not be able to keep his promise.

The trial lasted a little less than six weeks. First, the prosecution team presented its case. Over the course of eighteen days, one hundred and thirty-seven witnesses contributed to the prosecution's account of the events that led to the Oklahoma City bombing. According to government attorneys, McVeigh was motivated by a burning hatred of the federal government. He spent months gathering the ingredients to make an ammonium nitrate bomb and planning the attack. He rented the truck used in the bombing, and drove the truck to Oklahoma City. The government's case was strong and detailed, but it was not without flaws. No one testified to having seen McVeigh constructing the bomb, and no one had actually seen him at the scene of the disaster. Most of the prosecution's evidence was circumstantial (evidence that is based on circumstances rather than facts).

GUILTY!

Faced with a detailed timeline of McVeigh's activities prior to the bombing, defense lawyers needed to present an alternative account of their client's activities during the period leading up to the incident. But McVeigh's lawyers could offer no such proof. No friend, relative, or stranger was able to provide evidence that McVeigh was not in Oklahoma City on the day of the bombing. And McVeigh did not testify in his own defense. After just three and a half days of testimony, the defense rested its case. After closing arguments (summary statements by the defense and prosecuting attorneys), the seven men and five women of the jury were sequestered (secluded) while they decided the eleven charges of murder and conspiracy against McVeigh.

On June 2, 1997—after just twenty-three hours of discussions—the jury arrived at a verdict. The jurors returned to a courtroom packed with fifty bombing survivors and relatives of the victims who had died. McVeigh entered the courtroom smiling. None of his family was present. When the verdict was announced, he showed no emotion. McVeigh was found guilty of all eleven charges against him, including eight counts of first-degree murder of federal agents. Later that month, the jury decided on McVeigh's sentence. Each of the twelve jurors voted for the death penalty.

Sources for Further Reading

Annin, Peter, Tom Morgenthau, and Randy Collier. "Blowing Smoke." *Newsweek* (February 19, 1996), pp. 28–31.

Dead man waiting

In 1996, Congress implemented legal changes to speed up the execution of criminals on death row. But experts estimate that it will take four to six years to put McVeigh to death.

Gun money

The bombing of the Murrah building was an expensive undertaking. It involved purchasing thousands of pounds of fertilizer and other explosive agents. The bomber also had to pay storage, vehicle rental, and travel expenses. Federal investigators believe that the bombing was financed by the sale of guns—including stolen weapons.

On November 5, 1994, Roger E. Moore, an Arkansas gun dealer, was robbed by a man wearing camouflage battle dress and a black ski mask. Armed with a shotgun, the man taped Moore's legs and feet and swept through the house, stealing pistols and rifles, gold, silver, and cash. The robber escaped with $60,000 in cash and valuables.

When FBI agents raided the home of Terry Nichols, they found a number of things that had been taken from Moore during the robbery—including guns, gold coins, a bag of money, and the key to Moore's safety deposit box. Federal investigators believed that McVeigh and Nichols masterminded the robbery and used the money to finance the bombing.

Bragg, Rick. "McVeigh Guilty on All Counts in the Oklahoma City Bombing; Jury to Weigh Death Penalty." *The New York Times* (June 3, 1997), p. A1

Collins, James. "The Merits of the Case." *Time* (June 9, 1997), pp. 28–29.

Kifner, John. "U.S. Case Against 2d Defendant May Not Go as Smoothly." *The New York Times* (June 3, 1997), p. A19.

Stickney, Brandon M. *All-American Monster: The Unauthorized Biography of Timothy McVeigh*. Buffalo, NY: Prometheus Books, 1996.

Terry, Don. "Steel with Soft Surface." *The New York Times* (June 3, 1997), p. A19.

Thomas, Evan et al. "Inside the Plot." *Newsweek* (June 5, 1995), pp. 24–27.

Thomas, Evan et al. "The Plot." *Newsweek* (May 8, 1995), pp. 28–34.

Thomas, Jo. "Six Weeks, One Theory." *The New York Times* (June 3, 1997), p. A1.

Thomas, Jo. "Verdict Is Cheered." *The New York Times* (June 3, 1997), p. A1.

Watson, Russell and Evan Thomas. "Cleverness—and Luck." *Newsweek* (May 1, 1995), pp. 30–35.

Diana Oughton

Born: January 26, 1942
Died: March 6, 1970

Once a promising young student and social activist, Diana Oughton became increasingly radical during the political turmoil of the Vietnam era. Never identified as a prominent terrorist, she died in a bomb factory of the Weathermen—a terrorist organization to which she belonged.

A SOLID FAMILY

Born on January 26, 1942, Oughton was the first of her parents' four daughters. She was raised in Dwight, Illinois, a small farming community in the northern part of the state. Oughton's family was respected for its history of social consciousness. Her father's great-great-grandfather founded the Keeley Institute for alcoholics. And her mother's great-grandfather, W. D. Boyce, was responsible for establishing the American Boy Scouts. Oughton's father, James Oughton, turned to the restaurant business after completing an Ivy League education. Conservative and Episcopalian, the Oughton family stood out in the community of just over three thousand people.

Oughton enjoyed an upper-middle class childhood. She swam, played tennis, and was an accomplished horseback rider. She learned to play the flute and piano. The Oughton family ate dinner together in the evening, and the children were included in discussions on an equal basis with adults. Even as a child, Oughton expressed strong opinions. Her father later remem-

Students for a Democratic Society

Although the members of the Students for a Democratic Society (SDS) played a minor role in demonstrations against American involvement in the Vietnam War as early as September 1963, its major focus during the first half of the 1960s was on domestic issues (problems within the United States). In 1963, the organization began its Economic Research and Action Project (ERAP) to enlist the involvement of the urban poor in the democratic system. The project was established in ten cities, among them Baltimore, Maryland; Boston, Massachusetts; Chicago, Illinois; Cleveland, Ohio; Newark, New Jersey; and Philadelphia, Pennsylvania. Most ERAP projects were short-lived, although new ones sprang up as soon as old ones died.

In late 1964, while leaders of the first generation of SDS were still involved in grassroots domestic issues, the second generation was already starting to focus on the Vietnam War. They planned an antiwar campaign that included an April 1965 protest march in Washington, D.C.

The bombing of North Vietnam, which began in February 1965, triggered an increase in opposition to the war. In December 1964, SDS had hoped to draw 2,000 demonstrators to its April march. As many as 25,000 protesters

bered that she was an independent thinker who always had her own ideas—about anything from movies to how animals should be treated.

A SOCIAL CONSCIENCE

As a young woman, Oughton attended the Madeira School in Greenway, Virginia. Later, she was enrolled at Bryn Mawr College, an exclusive women's school, where she began to take an interest in community affairs and social injustices. She became active in voter registration, helping underprivileged individuals register to vote. Many activists then and now see voter registration as the first step in addressing the social problems of the poor and of minority groups who are not well-represented in political issues.

Oughton also began to tutor underprivileged students. Over the course of two years, she took a train at night to a ghetto area in Philadelphia, Pennsylvania, where she tutored two junior high school boys. The experience was eye-opening. Oughton's younger sister, Carol, later told *Time* magazine, "I remember how showed up. SDS had been growing steadily, from 250 members in December 1960, to 2,500 in December 1964. As the war rose to new heights, so did SDS membership. By October 1965, 25,000 people claimed SDS membership.

The original members of the SDS believed that the political system could be forced to reform itself. But many of the newcomers to the organization in 1965 and 1966 lacked that faith. As the war heated up, many members of the old guard began to agree. By late 1967, the SDS had entered a new phase, focusing on resistance to the war and military draft. The new SDS leadership dismissed plans for the antiwar demonstrations at the 1968 Democratic National Convention as insufficiently revolutionary. The small number of SDS members who went to Chicago played a role in heading up the demonstrations. They came away believing that the young people of America were ready for revolution on the streets.

Although the SDS no longer kept careful records, its membership was estimated between 80,000 and 100,000. But just as the SDS should have been at the height of its influence, two rival groups began to battle for its control. In June 1969, at an SDS convention, the Weathermen and Progressive Labor Party—who followed the Chinese Communism of Mao Tsetung (1893–1976)—split the organization in two.

incredulous [disbelieving] she was that a seventh- or eighth-grade child couldn't read, didn't even know the alphabet."

Oughton spent her junior year in Germany, as a student at the University of Munich. There she chose to turn away from the trappings of a privileged existence. She pedaled around town on a bicycle instead of hiring a taxicab. And when she traveled, she chose inexpensive rooms over expensive hotels.

Living in Guatemala

When a football player from Princeton University proposed marriage to her, Oughton turned him down. She said that she was not ready to marry because she had too many things to do. After graduating from Bryn Mawr, she joined the American Friends Service Committee, an organization devoted to social relief. After taking an intensive course in the Spanish language, Oughton traveled to the Latin American country of Guatemala, where she taught Guatemalan Indians the language she had recently learned. (Many of them spoke only a native dialect. Their inability to speak and understand Spanish, the official

Bill Ayers.

language of Guatemala, made it even more difficult to rise out of the poverty and oppression in which much of the country lived.)

Stationed in the town of Chichicastenango, Oughton was shocked by the area's terrible poverty—and by the bitter hatred between the large class of poor people and the very small group of wealthy individuals. What's more, she was disturbed by the fact that the United States supported the Guatemalan regime—a government she considered to be unjust and oppressive.

RADICAL IDEAS

After she returned to the United States, Oughton enrolled at the University of Michigan in order to earn a teaching certificate. As a student, she participated in the Children's Community School, an experimental school for children ages four to eight. The school offered an open and informal approach to education, but the institution collapsed in 1968, when its funding disappeared.

While involved in the Children's Community School, Oughton met Bill Ayers, who later became one of the prominent leaders of a political group known as the Students for a Democratic Society (SDS). Oughton joined the SDS and became more political and radical (revolutionary). When she discussed politics with her father, she argued in favor of revolutionary approaches to social problems—approaches that often involved violence. Oughton's relationship with her family became increasingly strained. Convinced that his daughter had become completely carried away with radical ideas, her father and the rest of the Oughton family lost touch with Diana.

JOINS RADICAL GROUP

For two years, beginning in 1968, Oughton's family knew next to nothing about her whereabouts. The legal establishment, on the other hand, became increasingly familiar with Oughton's activities. In 1969, the SDS had splintered into sepa-

The Weathermen

By 1970, small groups of extremists turned from protests to street riots and terrorist violence. In 1969, the Weathermen formed a radical splinter group from the Students for a Democratic Society (SDS). The words "You don't need a weatherman to know which way the wind blows," taken from a Bob Dylan song, "Subterranean Homesick Blues," were the source of the Weathermen's name. The Weathermen organized street riots in Chicago and attacked federal buildings around the country, calling for revolution in the United States. In October of that year, the Weathermen group stormed through Chicago streets, destroying property and beating up people who got in their way—supposedly to protest the trial of the organizers of the Chicago demonstrations at the Democratic National Convention in August 1968, and to "bring the war back home."

But the Weathermen's "days of rage" rampage failed to mobilize the large numbers of young Chicagoans who had turned out for the defendants' protest marches. The Weathermen suffered more injuries and financial damage than their targets. Two hundred Weathermen were arrested.

In June 1970, the Weathermen bombed the New York City police headquarters, inflicting substantial damage. They took credit for seven other bombings from 1970 to 1972. Weathermen bombings destroyed the army's mathematics lab center in Madison, Wisconsin, killing one person. Another bomb blew up part of the U.S. Capitol.

Many Americans were frightened by the violence—and violent words—of the Weathermen. By 1970 they had almost no public support. On March 6, 1970, the explosion of a Weathermen bomb factory in the basement of a New York townhouse killed three members, and the discovery of antipersonnel explosives in their arsenal further destroyed their limited base of support. Charged with several offenses, the Weathermen went underground. Some took on new identities. Others joined forces with Black Panther Party members who were in exile in Algeria.

rate camps. Oughton and Ayers joined the most violent and extreme group of radicals, known as the Weathermen. As a member of the Weathermen, Oughton established a criminal record. Caught passing out pamphlets to high school students, she was arrested in Flint, Michigan. In Chicago, Illinois, she was arrested for raids against the police that were known as the Weathermen's "days of rage."

In December 1969, a small group of Weathermen held a secret meeting in Flint. The meeting reportedly ended in a plan

The Democratic National Convention

In Chicago, Illinois, during the Democratic National Convention of 1968, city police beat thousands of demonstrators protesting the war in Vietnam. At the time, an official government report labeled the incident a "police riot." The televised pictures of the Chicago police clubbing demonstrators angered many young Americans—some of whom turned to violence in response to the brutal police action. A poll taken after the convention, revealed that 368,000 young people called themselves revolutionaries.

to begin a wave of terrorist bombings. The Detroit police claimed that Oughton was present at that meeting.

Although bomb threats worried the country throughout the following year, Oughton was never accused in any bombing or conspiracy to plot a bombing. On March 6, 1970, a house on 11th Street in Manhattan, New York, was destroyed by a bomb. The address was determined to be a bomb factory where the Weathermen put together the explosives they intended to use in bombings. As police scoured the ruins of the shattered house, they concluded that three people had died in the explosion. Having found a severed finger, they identified one of the victims as twenty-eight-year-old Diana Oughton.

Sources for Further Reading

Franks, L. and T. Powers. "Destruction of Diana." *Reader's Digest* (November 1970), pp. 49–58.

"Memories of Diana." *Time* (March 30, 1970), p. 21.

Powers, Thomas. *Diana: The Making of a Terrorist.* Boston: Houghton Mifflin, 1971.

"Seeds of Terror." *The New York Times Magazine* (November 22, 1981), pp. 34–38.

Index

Italic type indicates volume number;
boldface *indicates main entries and their page numbers;*
(ill.) indicates illustration.

train robbery in Georgia *1:* 176

train robbery in U.S. *3:* 344

use of California's gas chamber *3:* 435

woman executed *1:* 177

woman tried for major crime *3:* 399

Fitzgerald, F. Scott *1:* 97

Five Points Gang *1:* 13–15

"The Fixer." *See* Rothstein, Arnold

Flamingo Hotel *1:* 62

Flegenheimer, Arthur. *See* Schultz, Dutch

Fleischer, Louis *1:* 53

Fleisher, Harry *1:* 53, 54 (ill.)

Flesch, Oscar *1:* 97

Fletcher, Eddie *1:* 55 (ill.), 57

Florida Land Scam *2:* 295

Floyd, Pretty Boy *1:* 134

Ford, Bob *3:* 392 (ill.), 393

Ford, Charles *3:* 392

Ford, Henry *1:* 122. *See also* Automobiles

Ford, Robert *3:* 392

Forrest, Nathan Bedford *3:* 333

Fort Sumner *3:* 350

Fortier, Michael *2:* 322

"Forty-niners" *3:* 338. *See also* California gold rush

42 Gang *1:* 3, 5, 28, 30

Foster, Marcus *1:* 158

Fox, Richard *3:* 401

Francis, James *1:* 166

Frasier 1: 161

Freeh, Louis J. *2:* 316

Friends of the Soviet Union *2:* 232

Frog Hollow Gang *3:* 452

Fuchs, Klaus *2:* 237

Fulton-Rockaway Boys *1:* 35

Fusco, Tony *1:* 80

G

Galente, Carmine *1:* 26

Galione, Ralphie *1:* 37

Gallows *3:* 494. *See also* Death penalty

Gambino, Carlo *1:* **21–27,** 21 (ill.), 22 (ill.), 33, 37

Gambino family chart *1:* 22 (ill.)

Gamblers. *See* Racketeers and gamblers

Gandil, Chick *1:* 97

Garcia, Andy *1:* 33

Garlic-tipped bullets *3:* 425

Garrett, John *3:* 354

Garrett, Pat *3:* 350, 351 (ill.), 352–353

Geaquenta, Mack *1:* 85

Genna, Angelo *3:* 424, 426, 445, 467

Genna, Antonio *3:* 424

Genna, Jim *3:* 424, 429

Genna, Mike *3:* 424, 427

Genna, Pete *3:* 424, 429

Genna, Sam *3:* 424, 429

Genna, Tony *3:* 425, 428

The Genna Brothers *1:* 87; *3:* 420, **424–429,** 445

Genovese, Vito *1:* 23–24, 73; *2:* 232; *3:* 455

"Gentleman Johnnie." *See* Dillinger, John

George I *3:* 481

Giancana, Antonino *1:* 28

Giancana, Carlo *1:* 4

Giancana, Gilormo. *See* Giancana, Sam

Giancana, Sam *1:* 3–5, **28–34,** 28 (ill.), 31 (ill.)

Gibbet cage *3:* 489

Gibbs, Charles *3:* **492–495,** 492 (ill.)

Gigante, Vincent *1:* 73

Gillis, Lester. *See* Nelson, Baby Face

Ginter, Leonard *2:* 312–313

Ginter, Norma *2:* 312–313

Giunta, Joseph *1:* 19

The Godfather 1: 24, 25

The Godfather, Part II 1: 52

Goebbels, Joseph *1:* 59

Goering, Hermann *1:* 59

Gold *3:* 338–339. *See also* California gold rush

Gold, Harry *2:* 236–239

Goodwin Act (1864) *1:* 174

Gopher Gang *1:* 68; *3:* 437

Gordon, Waxey *1:* 76

Gotti, Frank *1:* 37

Gotti, John *1:* **35–40,** 35 (ill.), 39 (ill.)

Gotti, Victoria *1:* 38

Graham, William B. *See* Curly Bill

Grant, Ulysses S. *2:* 247 (ill.), 248

Gravano, Salvatore "Sammy the Bull" *1:* 39 (ill.), 40

"Graveyard of the Atlantic" *3:* 479

The Great Gatsby 1: 97

Great Michigan Free Land Swindle *2:* 299

Great Northern Flyer train *3:* 372

Green, Eddie *1:* 140, 143

Greenglass, David *2:* 236, 239

Greenglass, Ethel. *See* Rosenberg, Ethel

Grishin, Boris A. *2:* 226

Guerrilla warfare *3:* 388

Gulf War *2:* 316

Gunness, Belle *1:* **144–150,** 144 (ill.), 147 (ill.)

Gunness, Peter *1:* 145

Gunslingers. *See* Bandits and gunslingers

Gusenberg, Frank *1:* 18 *3:* 427

Gusenberg, Pete *1:* 18

H

Hamer, Frank *1:* 126

Hamilton, John *1:* 136, 140

Hamilton, Ray *1:* 123, 126

Hamm, William A. Jr. *1:* 110; *3:* 462

Handshake murder *3:* 421, 426

"Hanover Hacker." *See* Hess, Marcus

Harrington "Alkali Jim" *1:* 172

Harris, Emily *1:* 160–162

Harris, Maury *2:* 281

L

M